Sunset

Roses

By the Editors

of Sunset Books

and

Sunset Magazine

Impatient

Lane Publishing Co. ◆ *Menlo Park, California*

Milestone

Cover: From elegantly pointed buds to full and shapely open flowers, aptly named 'Touch of Class' epitomizes hybrid tea beauty. And as its 1986 AARS award testifies, another sterling quality is all-around performance. For details, see page 38. Photography by Ells Marugg.

Editor, Sunset Books: Elizabeth L. Hogan

Second printing January 1990

Research & Text
Philip Edinger

Developmental Editor
Scott Atkinson

Coordinating Editor
Suzanne Normand Mathison

Design
Joe di Chiarro

Illustrations
Rik Olson
Vernon Koski
Carol Etow

Photographers

Scott Atkinson: 1, 8 top right, 9 center, 25 bottom, 29, 31 top and bottom left, 38 right, 43 left, 51 bottom left. **Joyce Demits:** 7 top and bottom, 57 left, 60 left, 61 bottom left. **Philip Edinger:** 8 bottom right, 9 left. **Derek Fell:** 31 right, 32 right, 45 left, 62. **Gerald R. Fredrick:** 4. **Harry Haralambou:** 25 top, 46 center. **Pamela Harper:** 23 bottom, 44 bottom right. **Saxon Holt:** 17, 49 left. **Horticultural Photography:** 18, 44 top right, 45 center, 46 right, 47 center, 48 center, 56 bottom left. **Russell Lamb:** 34 right. **Michael Landis:** 22 left, 49 center. **Jack McDowell:** 32 left, 34 center, 40 left. **John C. MacGregor IV:** 7 center and right, 8 left, 12 right, 13 right, 50 right, 58 left and top right, 59 top left and right, 61 right. **Stephen Marley:** 49 right, 63 left. **Ells Marugg:** 9 right, 12 left, 13 left, 19 bottom, 30, 33 center and right, 34 left, 35 left and right, 36, 37 right, 38 left, 40 center, 41, 42 left and right, 43 right, 44 left and center, 45 right, 46 left, 47 left and right, 48 left, 50 left and center, 51 right, 52 top row, 53 top left and bottom row, 55 top row, middle row, and bottom right, 57 top and bottom right, 60 right, 63 center and right, 64. **Norman A. Plate:** 52 bottom left. **Bill Ross:** 55 bottom left. **Teri Sandison:** 22 right. **Chad Slattery:** 27 top. **Michael Thompson:** 5, 23 top, 24, 28. **Darrow M. Watt:** 12 center, 16. **Tom Wyatt:** 2, 19 top, 20, 21, 27 bottom, 31 center, 33 left, 35 center, 37 left and center, 39, 40 right, 42 center, 48 top and bottom right, 51 top left, 52 bottom right, 53 top right, 56 top left and right, 58 bottom right, 59 bottom left, 61 top left.

Friends of the Rose

Writings about the rose and its culture extend back thousands of years—a testimony to the esteem in which the rose has been held throughout recorded civilization. In contrast, this book is a relative newcomer to the subject, its first edition having appeared in 1955. Our advantage as a newcomer, though, is the opportunity to benefit from the research that has preceded us.

The foundation for this edition was laid in 1973. Since that time, the material it presents has been reviewed, modified, and polished by a veritable "who's who" of contemporary rosedom, to whom we express our gratitude: Dr. R. C. Allen, Tucson, Arizona; David H. Berg, Bloomfield, Connecticut; Edwin A. Birge, Carrollton, Georgia; Charles P. Dawson, Simpsonville, Kentucky; Fred Edmunds, Wilsonville, Oregon; George Haight, San Jose, California; Don Herzog, Sebastopol, California; Muriel Humenick, Diamond Springs, California; Rudy Kalmbach, Portland, Oregon; Joseph Klima, Kentfield, California; Frank J. Lacoma, Omaha, Nebraska, Ross V. Lahr, Littleton, Colorado; John C. MacGregor IV, San Marino, California; Dr. C. A. Rohrer, Winona, Minnesota; Helene Schoen, Vancouver, Washington; Carson Scoggins, Shreveport, Louisiana; Dorothy Stemler, Watsonville, California; John van Barneveld, La Habra, California; Howard Walters, Houston, Texas; Miriam Wilkins, El Cerrito, California; and Barbara Worl, Menlo Park, California.

For their valuable assistance in preparing this edition, our thanks go to Daryl Johnson, Portland, Oregon; Clair G. Martin III, San Marino, California; Stephen C. Scanniello, Brooklyn, New York; Marian Thomson, Cedar Rapids, Iowa; and once again Howard Walters, Houston, Texas.

We also thank the American Rose Society for reviewing our manuscript.

Among those who graciously allowed us to photograph their gardens, we would like to thank Michael Bates, John Dallas, Ed Kaptur, and Joseph Mammino. Finally, we extend special thanks to JoAnn Masaoka Van Atta for styling some of the photographs, Marianne Lipanovich for location scouting, and Rebecca LaBrum for her careful editing of the manuscript.

Contents

Special Features

*Modern roses combine in a fragrant garden
potpourri. Shown are creamy pink
hybrid tea 'Sheer Bliss' at center and left;
orange-toned grandiflora 'New Year'; and, at
bottom, pink shrub rose 'Bonica '82'.*

Introducing the Queen

Just a casual glance is enough to explain why the rose has long been called the "queen of flowers." Yet this title was bestowed by the Greek poet Sappho over 2,500 years ago, long before roses had attained their present-day refinement. Even in ancient times, the simple rose must have had a regal quality that set it apart from other flowers. But today's roses have inherited more from their revered ancestors than the concrete characteristics of basic flower form and leaf shape. As the worldwide love of roses attests, they are also heirs to a special regard and respect stretching far back in time.

In the following pages, you'll find a brief sketch of rose history, including descriptions of the various types

Salet

that have enchanted cultures both ancient and modern—and contributed to the evolution of a flower universally acknowledged as "queen."

Though Sappho coined the lasting phrase, she is not the only ancient writer to have mentioned roses. References appear in Homer's Iliad and Odyssey; the historian Herodotus wrote of Phrygian King Midas' rose garden. In the 4th century B.C., the philosopher Theophrastus recorded botanical descriptions of contemporary roses and remarked that the flowers were then grown in Egypt as well as in Greece. At about the same time—but thousands of miles to the east—Confucius noted extensive rose plantings in the Peking Imperial Gardens.

By the time Roman civilization gained preeminence in the Mediterranean basin, roses were familiar in much of the territory. But the Roman culture, more than any other before it, popularized, exalted, and *used* the fragrant blossoms. Roses decorated parties, weddings, and funerals; on festival days and other important occasions, rose petals were strewn in the streets, and statues and monuments were wreathed in the flowers. Rose-draped warriors departed for battle in rose-adorned shields and chariots. In fact, roses pervaded nearly all aspects of upper-class life: wealthy Romans could bathe in rose water, wear rose garlands, eat confections made of rose petals, and sip rose wine. If ailing, they could take medications prepared from rose petals, hips, or seeds. (Given the high vitamin C content of rose hips, it seems likely that at least some of these medicines were beneficial!) Thanks to such widespread use, commercial rose growing became a profitable Roman industry.

The early Christian church, ascending as Rome was declining, adopted the rose as a symbol for survivors of religious persecution; a white rose often symbolized the Immaculate Conception of the Virgin Mary. "Rosary," originally meaning simply "rose garden," later named the series of prayers related to the life of Christ and the Virgin. The rose's role in Christian symbolism is perhaps most magnificently expressed, however, in the stained glass "rose window"—a standard component of medieval cathedrals.

From the earliest days of chivalry, roses were a favored motif in heraldry (a legacy, perhaps, of the rose-bedecked Roman shields and chariots). Beginning with Edward I in 1272, several English monarchs took the rose as their badge. Such usage gave the Wars of the Roses their name: the conflict involved the houses of York and Lancaster, whose emblems were a white and red rose, respectively.

The dawn of modern rose growing

During the nearly 1,000 years between the fall of the Roman Empire and the dawn of the Renaissance, the western European interest in rose culture was kept alive in the hundreds of Christian monasteries scattered over the continent. But only fairly recently was the stage set for the development of modern rose growing. The foundations were laid around 1800, with the building blocks going into place during the course of the century.

From the viewpoint of modern rose culture, nothing is historically more significant than the Empress Josephine's passion for roses. The wife of France's Napoleon I used her extensive resources to pursue her hobby of collecting and maintaining all the rose species and hybrids then known in the western world. Begun in 1804, her collection at the imperial château Malmaison reached its zenith 10 years later, by which time it contained about 250 different roses. So famous and respected was Josephine's endeavor that it transcended even international animosities. The British, then at war with France, permitted plants found on captured French ships to be sent on to Malmaison. And when the Napoleonic Wars ended in 1815, occupying British troops were ordered to protect the Malmaison garden from harm.

To preserve her treasured collection for posterity, the Empress summoned a group of artists to Malmaison. Among them was Pierre-Joseph Redouté—the "Raphael of the flowers"—whose watercolor paintings were later published in a three-volume work, *Les Roses,* accompanied with botanical descriptions prepared by Claude Antoine Thory. Even now, Redouté's paintings remain unsurpassed in both beauty and detail.

Fortunately, a number of the Malmaison roses—plus later representatives of the types—are still grown today, so that modern gardeners can appreciate first hand the beauty that enchanted Josephine and inspired Redouté. The bulk of the collection comprised species, selected forms, and natural hybrids of roses from Europe and the Near East. Aside from the Autumn Damask, they all had but one annual flowering period in spring. Botanists and horticulturists of the day separated them into several distinct classes (described below) based on ancestry and appearance. Collectively, these classes are known today as old European roses and are included among the "old garden roses" that preceded the modern hybrid tea class.

Gallica roses. More than half of Josephine's 250-odd roses were gallicas—varieties, and in some cases hybrids, of *Rosa gallica.* Known also as the French rose, the species grows wild in western Europe. Its flowers are pink to light red, but the hybrid color range is wider, extending from rich maroon and dark red shades through light pink and a number of striped combinations. As a group, the gallicas are notably fragrant and very hardy, adaptable, and vigorous. Typical varieties are compact and upright, with dark green, somewhat rough-textured leaves; the canes are nearly smooth, bearing just a few small thorns.

Damask roses. Josephine had only eight of these roses. They were a somewhat mysterious group: their place of origin and, most importantly, how one of them possessed the ability to flower more than once yearly, were subjects of some debate. What was called *Rosa damascena* (the specific name is taken from Damascus, Syria) seems to have been brought west by Phoenician traders or Greek colonists, if not by the Egyptians. Romans knew the repeat-flowering Autumn Damask as the "Rose of Paestum" (or of Cyrinae or Carthage), and its likeness appears on frescoes in Pompeii. Many centuries later, Spanish missionaries brought it to North America, where it is known as the "Rose of Castile."

In growth habit, the damasks vary from fairly compact to rangy or sprawling. The foliage is often grayish and softly downy; the canes tend to be thorny, frequently carrying both large thorns and smaller prickles. The flowers, typically white or pink, are legendary for their fragrance: even today, acres of a summer damask type are grown in Bulgaria to produce the petals from which attar of roses is extracted.

Alba roses. Only nine alba roses grew in Josephine's garden. Of the early forms of *Rosa alba* and its later hybrids, just a few remain in cultivation—but these include some of the most valuable old roses for garden use. The original

Fantin-Latour (Centifolia)

Félicité Parmentier (Alba) *Autumn Damask (Damask)* *Tuscany Superb (Gallica)*

◆ Old European Roses

The flowers shown on this page belong to the classes of old garden roses developed in Europe and the southern Mediterranean region before 1800. Aside from the Autumn Damask, these are selections or hybrids of European species and bloom heavily just once a year, in spring. All are fine flowering shrubs, still available for planting in modern gardens.

albas were natural hybrids between the damask rose and a white form of the dog rose (*Rosa canina*); the combination sweetened the damask parent's tangy perfume and produced long-lived, sparsely thorned plants of vigorous, upright habit and exceptional disease resistance. All the albas flower only in spring, with single to very double blossoms in delicate tints of pink or white that are beautifully set off by the plentiful gray-green foliage. Most of these roses tolerate some shade, and their highly adaptable growth suits them to use as self-supporting shrubs, as "climbers" attached to walls or fences, or, more closely pruned, as bedding roses.

Centifolia roses. About an eighth of the Malmaison collection consisted of varieties and hybrids of *Rosa centifolia*, a species originating from a back-cross between a form of *Rosa alba* and its damask parent. Often called "cabbage roses," the centifolias have a great many petals (sometimes 100 or more) packed into each flower; a typical blossom has large outer petals that, as the flower opens, cradle the multitude of smaller petals within. Colors include white and all shades of pink, but none have the rich reds found in the gallicas. Many varieties have lax, thorny canes that arch or sprawl with the weight of the blossoms.

Though the centifolias have only one flowering season, they have two claims to fame. One is their intensely sweet fragrance; they are still the main source of true rose essence

for the French perfume industry. The other is their inclination to produce mutations of various sizes, colors, and forms, among them the moss roses and some of the first miniature garden roses.

Moss roses. Anomalies of the rose kingdom, these arose quite by chance and are beloved for their charming difference, but have contributed nothing to the development of other classes. The "moss" in the name refers to a dense coating of balsam-scented glands that covers the unopened buds, the flower stems, and sometimes even the leaflets. In Josephine's time, mutations were the sole source of moss roses; only in later years were some achieved through hybridization.

The first moss roses appeared, perhaps around 1700, as a mutation of *Rosa centifolia*. Called Common Moss (or *Rosa centifolia muscosa*), it bears clear pink flowers crammed with petals that open around a green central "eye." 'Chapeau de Napoleon' (1827), also known as Crested Moss, is another centifolia mutation, with qualities partway between true centifolia and true moss. Its pink blooms are typical centifolia, but the green calyces covering the buds are neither smooth nor "mossy"—instead, they are elaborately fringed. Moss rose types have also developed from damask rose mutations, but a particular moss rose's parentage is easily discerned by touch: a centifolia moss is soft, while a damask moss is distinctly prickly.

19th-century rosemania

Malmaison was the most important rose collection of the early 19th century, at its peak at a time when horticultural horizons were expanding rapidly. The British, French, and Dutch were establishing firm footholds in the Orient—a part of the world largely closed to western European contact until the 17th and 18th centuries. Through the East India Companies of these three countries, increasing numbers of unfamiliar plants were sent to individuals and botanical gardens in Europe. Among these were four roses destined to revolutionize the garden rose as it was then known.

The first east Asian roses reached western Europe in the 18th century. Known to Europeans as 'Parson's Pink China' (now commonly called 'Old Blush') and 'Slater's Crimson China', they were both selected forms of *Rosa chinensis* that had been grown for centuries by the Chinese. Their clustered, smallish flowers may have suffered by comparison to the opulent European roses, but the China types had one undeniable point in their favor: they flowered from spring until stopped by frost.

Both 'Parson's Pink China' and 'Slater's Crimson China' were in the Malmaison collection, as was another treasure which reached Europe from eastern Asia in 1810: 'Hume's Blush Tea-scented China'. Too late for Josephine, though, was the closely related 'Park's Yellow Tea-scented China', which arrived in England in 1824. As the "China" in their names implies, these two last roses derive in part from *Rosa chinensis,* but their ancestry also includes *Rosa gigantea,* a rampant climber from the Himalayan foothills. "Tea-scented" simply describes the fragrance: the scent is reminiscent of a good-quality Chinese black tea.

Compared to the two earlier China roses, the tea-scented types had larger flowers on larger, woodier (and more cold-tender) plants; today, we would recognize them as the first roses to resemble modern hybrid teas.

Until the time of Josephine, development of new roses was largely in the hands of Nature. But the Malmaison collection brought together a large number of very different roses from widely separated geographical regions—an assembly that would never have been found in one place under natural circumstances. In seedling plantings, altogether new roses began cropping up, most importantly

♦ 19th Century: The Asian Influence

Thanks to the arrival of China roses in the western world, 19th-century roses differed significantly from the "old" European kinds. Cross-breeding with the Chinas altered flower style and plant habit, and—most importantly—gave the new hybrid groups the ability to flower more than once annually. The stage was set for the emergence of our modern roses.

Rose du Roi (Portland)

Souvenir de la Malmaison (Bourbon)

Cramoisi Supérieur (China)

hybrids of European roses with China and tea-scented China sorts.

Spurred on by the Malmaison collection and excited by hybrids from hitherto untried parentages, nurserymen began to pursue rose breeding in earnest. The result was a number of separate (but related) groups that were the latest horticultural word at the time. Among the numerous 19th-century hybrids appeared—unheralded—the first hybrid teas, the class that now dominates our rose gardens.

Many of the last century's roses are available today from commercial old-rose growers. Following is a guide to the principal classes.

China roses. In Europe, roses that bloomed all year (frost permitting) were a novelty that had important consequences for rose growing. Interest in the new types inspired gardeners to plant countless seeds from 'Parson's Pink China' and 'Slater's Crimson China' and encouraged the import of more plants and seeds from China and India. The net result was a sizable group of everblooming roses that, like the original types, produced clusters of small to medium-size flowers on bushy plants of modest stature.

Colors included white, pink shades, and red—the red shades often particularly luminous.

Portland roses. Beginning around 1800, the first new group of hybrids between the old European roses and the new Chinese introductions emerged. Their ancestries vary, but all seem to have been derived at least from the Autumn Damask and the China roses. Though sometimes catalogued as damask perpetuals, they were almost always called Portland roses after their first representative, 'Duchess of Portland'. All Portlands were fairly short and shrubby; the best ones combined the rich red tones of China and gallica roses with increased doubleness from the centifolias. Portlands maintained some popularity for about 50 years, but were ultimately eclipsed by their own descendants, the hybrid perpetuals (page 11).

Bourbon roses. Despite the name, Bourbon roses did not originate in Kentucky—or in France. The type first appeared on the Isle of Bourbon (now Réunion) in the Indian Ocean off Madagascar. Cultivated fields on the island were often fenced with hedges of mixed roses, fre-

Mons. Tillier (Tea)   *Blush Noisette (Noisette)*   *Mrs. John Laing (Hybrid Perpetual)*

Societies: The Camaraderie of Rosemania

Most rose growers enjoy sharing their experiences with other enthusiasts, and rose societies offer a perfect forum for this kind of socializing. The three groups listed here will help put you in touch with gardeners all over North America, supply information through publications, conventions, and symposia, and direct you to local organizations for person-to-person advice.

American Rose Society

The American Rose Society (ARS) was founded in 1899 to foster research, spread information on all aspects of rose growing, and bring together the many individuals interested in roses. Today, the ARS holds two national conventions each year and prints a monthly magazine as well as an annual of 200 or more pages. Each annual includes a "Proof of the Pudding" feature: a compilation of nationwide evaluations of newer rose varieties. Society members also receive an annual pamphlet giving point-score ratings—derived from surveys of ARS members—for all roses currently grown in the United States.

Of special interest to novice rose growers is the ARS's Consulting Rosarian Program, a nationwide network of dedicated and experienced growers who can give you advice on the rose varieties and type of rose culture best suited to your region. These volunteer consultants will also help you contact local, regional, and state societies.

For information on ARS membership, write to: American Rose Society, P.O. Box 30,000, Shreveport, LA 71130.

Canadian Rose Society

Embracing the same goals as the American Rose Society, the Canadian Rose Society was established in 1913 to serve the needs of Canadian rose growers. Publications include quarterly journals and an annual; meetings and other activities are held at the national and regional levels. For details on membership, contact: Canadian Rose Society, Mrs. B. Hunter, 20 Portico Drive, Scarborough, Ontario M1G 3R3.

Heritage Roses Group

Devotees of old roses formed the Heritage Roses Group in 1975 to share their experiences—and even their roses. For $5 ($6 for Canadian residents), you'll receive an informative quarterly, "The Rose Letter." Subgroups foster interest within each region. Send dues to Miriam Wilkins, 925 Galvin Drive, El Cerrito, CA 94530.

quently including 'Parson's Pink China' and the Autumn Damask. According to one account, a seedling which was an obvious hybrid between these two roses was discovered by a visiting French botanist in 1819. From the seeds he sent back to King Louis Philippe's gardener in Paris came the original Bourbon rose—a semidouble deep pink that flowered repeatedly. The plants were vigorous and semi-climbing, with shiny green leaves and purple-tinted canes.

Many Bourbon hybrids were named and sold during the 1800s; the best of these retained the Bourbon foliage and plant characteristics, as well as the repeat flowering. Ironically, the important old Bourbon-China hybrid 'Gloire des Rosomanes'—one of the primary sources of red color in present-day hybrid teas—has persisted in countless gardens today, but as an understock for modern roses.

Noisette roses. While Josephine was building her collection at Malmaison, John Champneys, a rice planter in Charleston, South Carolina, raised a hybrid between 'Parson's Pink China' and *Rosa moschata,* the old autumn-blooming musk rose. The hybrid, which he named 'Champneys' Pink Cluster', was a vigorous climber producing huge clusters of small blush-pink flowers from spring until frost. Champneys' neighbor, Philippe Noisette, scion of a prominent French nursery family, planted seeds of Champneys' hybrid and sent the progeny to his brother in France. In 1817, 'Blush Noisette' was introduced and bestowed its name on a new class of climbing roses.

The early Noisette roses were shrubby, small-flowered, fairly hardy climbers with the constant bloom of the China roses, in colors ranging from white through pink to crimson and purple. European hybridizers crossed these small Noisettes with the larger-flowered teas, obtaining roses with bigger blossoms in an expanded color range including soft yellow, salmon, and buff, but with smaller clusters and considerably reduced hardiness. These large-flowered tea-Noisettes are vigorous climbers, eminently suited to the warmer regions where teas thrive.

Noisettes contributed to modern roses on two fronts. First, they furnished the musk element in the ancestry of the hybrid musk shrub roses (see page 12). Second (and more important), Noisettes entered into the development of yellow tea roses and thence into later hybrid teas.

Tea roses. This group derived from crosses between the two tea-scented Chinas ('Hume's Blush' and 'Park's Yellow'), the Noisettes, and the Bourbon roses. During the last half of the 19th century, the teas were the preeminent garden roses in climates where there was little winter chill to interfere with their inherently evergreen, evergrowing, virtually everblooming nature.

The tea palette encompasses pastel shades and combinations of pink, cream, buff, yellow, and white; the flower buds are long and tapered, frequently semipendant because of weak "necks" below the blossoms. In many individuals, the foliage is highly disease resistant. Often referred to as the "aristocrats of the rose world," tea roses left their flower form and overall refinement—and some of their intolerance of cold—as legacies to modern roses.

Hybrid perpetual roses. The first roses that could be classed as hybrid perpetuals made their appearance around 1838. From then until just after the turn of the century, the production of these roses occupied all rose breeders of any consequence; as a result, the group numbered over 3,000 members before being superseded by its offspring, the hybrid tea class (see below).

The hybrid perpetuals were the garden and cut-flower workhorses of the 19th century, particularly in cold-winter regions where the teas would not thrive. As the name implies, they were definitely hybrids, encompassing in their ancestries practically all the garden roses that had gone before them, but many were far from *perpetual* bloomers. The tendency was for a massive spring flowering, followed by scattered bloom for the rest of the year, or by a smaller autumn burst, or even by nothing at all until the next spring. The French called the class *hybrides rémontants*—"reblooming hybrids"—a more accurate description than "perpetuals."

Hybrid perpetuals generally bore large, full-petaled flowers, in a color range extending from white through all shades of pink and red to purple. But as the hybrid teas increased in number, the hybrid perpetuals lost favor because of three handicaps: limited color range, lack of a dependable perpetual-flowering inclination, and rampant growth habit. In floral beauty, the best old hybrid perpetuals are easily the equal of more modern roses.

Modern roses

The "modern" era of rose growing began in 1867, with the introduction of what is now designated the first hybrid tea rose—the class that dominates present-day rose gardens.

Hybrid tea roses. Despite their importance today, hybrid teas did not arrive on the rose scene with great fanfare; they crept in almost imperceptibly. This entry has led to some controversy over which rose was really the first of the class—but many modern rosarians agree that 'La France', introduced in 1867, provided the earliest indication that a truly new rose type was on the horizon. Some years later, as similar sorts appeared, the term "hybrid tea" was coined, and a new era was underway.

The original hybrid teas were direct crosses of hybrid perpetual and tea roses, and their characteristics fall midway between those of the parent types. They are smaller and bushier than hybrid perpetuals, and flower throughout the growing season in all climates; but they are less everblooming than the teas, with stiffer, more sparsely foliaged canes. Hardiness varies, though nearly all hybrid teas tolerate colder temperatures than the tea roses do.

Until 1900, the color range in the new class was the same as that found among the hybrid perpetuals, with the addition of creamy yellow tints from the teas. The onset of the 20th century, however, marked a turning point for hybrid teas in particular and, indeed, for roses in general: it saw the introduction of Joseph Pernet's 'Soleil d'Or' ("Golden Sun"). Derived from 'Persian Yellow' (a double form of the Austrian brier rose, *Rosa foetida*) and a purple-red hybrid perpetual, this was the first repeat-blooming, reasonably hardy, large-flowered, deep yellow bush rose. (Yellow teas did exist, but they were tender plants, and the flower color often faded to nearly white.) Though not itself a hybrid tea in either appearance or ancestry, 'Soleil d'Or' did remarkable things when crossed with one. It infused exciting new blood into the old, familiar classes of white, pink, and red roses, giving rise to an entirely new palette of colors: bright golden yellow, flame, copper, soft orange, and bicolors of yellow and almost any other color.

The exotic new hues did not come without a price, however. Beside its vibrant color, the *Rosa foetida* parent passed along a tendency toward poorly formed blooms and lustrous foliage particularly susceptible to black spot. Another less than desirable inheritance was a definite resentment of pruning: if the canes were severely cut back, either by design or as a consequence of harsh winter weather, the plants often died.

For a number of years, the hybrid tea–'Soleil d'Or' crosses formed a separate subclass called pernetianas, but by the 1930s, they had been crossed so extensively with hybrid teas that the latter group absorbed them. Today, the glorious pernetiana colors have permeated all modern rose classes as has the pernetiana dislike of pruning. And curiously enough, it is pernetiana heritage that is responsible for most of the recent modern roses in shades of mauve, lavender, gray, tan, and brown.

Polyantha & floribunda roses. The earliest polyantha roses, derived from the Japanese *Rosa multiflora* and forms of *Rosa chinensis,* made their appearance in France at about the same time as the hybrid teas. The original polyanthas flowered constantly on short, compact plants, featuring blossoms about an inch across—not particularly impressive in form, but carried in such large clusters that a blooming plant might be literally covered with flowers.

Inevitably, the polyanthas were crossed with hybrid teas to develop plants that bloomed with polyantha profusion but had larger, better-formed flowers in a wider range of colors. Some records indicate that the first such hybrid was 'Gruss an Aachen', introduced in 1909. But credit goes to Denmark's Poulsen family for pursuing this line of breeding to obtain roses hardy enough for their northern European climate, as free-flowering as the polyanthas yet with bigger, individually beautiful blossoms.

It soon became evident that the polyantha-hybrid tea crosses would need a designation other than "polyantha" (or even "hybrid polyantha"): the larger flowers and bulkier, bushier plants set them apart from their polyantha parents. Finally, in the 1940s, the term "floribunda" was coined.

Through repeated crossings with the hybrid teas, floribundas have undergone a continuing transition from the original types, which bore single or semidouble blossoms in large clusters. Modern floribundas are available with the best hybrid tea form, in all the hybrid tea colors. In fact, some differ from hybrid teas only in their cluster-flowering habit.

Ophelia　　　　　　　　　*Belinda*　　　　　　　　　*Pink Gruss an Aachen*

♦ 20th-century Progress

The hybrid teas have dominated 20th century rose gardens, and one of the most influential in modern rose development has been 'Ophelia'. Shrub roses—hybrids of varied ancestry—are gaining popularity; shown here is 'Belinda'. Floribunda roses, heralded by 'Gruss an Aachen', stem from polyanthas crossed with hybrid teas. Miniature forms of the China rose founded the race of modern miniatures, represented by 'Rosemarin'. Colorful 'Picasso' illustrates the novel effect an untried species can have on a breeding program.

Grandiflora roses. To set apart the hybrid tea–floribunda hybrids that fit neither category, American rose growers coined the term "grandiflora." Though the name has been challenged (British rosarians refer to these roses as "floribundas, hybrid tea type"), the term aptly describes the plants so named. The bushes are usually larger and more vigorous than the average hybrid tea. Flowers may be as large as those of hybrid teas, but they are borne on fairly long stems within few-flowered clusters; consequently, grandifloras approach floribunda bloom production.

Miniature roses. All the old European rose types—gallicas, damasks, albas, centifolias, even mosses—have corresponding miniature forms. Though popular in the 18th century, these small-scale old roses lapsed into neglect after the introduction of the repeat-flowering miniature China rose (*Rosa chinensis minima*). The miniature China's exact origin is clouded, but the first plants reached Europe shortly after 1800—apparently imported from the island of Mauritius, a British possession in the Indian Ocean.

Miniatures have gone through two widely separated periods of development: first in the years 1820 to 1850, then in the years since 1930. The advent of polyantha roses (page 11) eclipsed the popularity of miniature Chinas in the last century, but interest in the type was rekindled when, around 1920, an attractive miniature China was discovered growing profusely in windowboxes in two small Swiss villages. Using this little rose ('Rouletii') and the 19th-

century miniature called 'Pompon de Paris', hybridizers have made extensive crosses with polyanthas, floribundas, and hybrid teas to produce the new race of miniatures. The results vary in flower and plant size, but typically replicate current hybrid tea colors and, frequently, flower form. Crosses of miniature roses with climbing types of *Rosa wichuraiana* derivations have produced a series of climbing and trailing miniatures.

Shrub roses. For many years, roses that fit none of the established classes were designated simply "shrub roses"; many of these were species hybrids that flowered only in spring and served as medium to large garden shrubs. Among the first recognizable groups of shrub roses were the hybrid musks, developed in England early in the 1900s and still widely available today. Newer types are also sold; since the mid-1900s, hybridizers in Europe, North America, and the Southern Hemisphere have devoted increasing attention to the shrub class. Their aim is to produce rugged, well-foliaged, easy-to-grow plants that both function as shrubs in the landscape and flower profusely for a long season, ideally bearing hybrid tea–type blossoms.

As the 1987 AARS award bestowed on 'Bonica '82' indicates, shrub roses have truly become an established part of the modern rose world. Taken as a whole, though, this "class" exhibits no uniformity: flowers may be single or double, small or large, on plants ranging from 3 feet to 8 feet tall or taller. Many are strictly mass-effect plants, but some

Rosmarin

Picasso

produce good flowers for cutting. In England, David Austin has taken an individual approach, breeding spring-flowering old garden roses with contemporary floribundas and hybrid teas; the result is a group of repeat-flowering "English Roses" which bear old-style flowers in both old and modern colors. Roses for ground cover planting are another variation on the shrub theme. These are dense, free-branching, ground-hugging plants that flower throughout the season; Japanese 'Nozomi' was the forerunner of the type.

Tomorrow's roses

Just as the 19th century saw the hybrid perpetual and tea roses rise to prominence, then gradually give way to their offspring, the 20th century will see the modern hybrid teas continue to improve and participate in the evolution of still newer types. As hybridizers search for new colors and patterns, previously underexplored or unused species are appearing in breeding programs. *Rosa foetida*, for example, has provided the more recent shades of lavender, brown, and purple as well as the range of yellow and flame tones described under "Hybrid tea roses" (page 11). From the Scotch brier, *Rosa spinosissima*, are derived various "hand-painted" roses—forecast by 'Picasso', in which color is seemingly brushed onto a white background, leaving a white central "eye."

Rose breeders everywhere strive for disease-proof foliage. In cold climates, an additional concern is the development of plants that will survive subzero winters with little or no damage to exposed canes. Various species have the desired characteristics; the problem has been to transfer that hardiness to plants bearing flowers of hybrid tea quality.

The development, by Wilhelm Kordes in Germany, of *Rosa kordesii*—an artificially created "species" derived from *Rosa rugosa* and *Rosa wichuraiana*—marked a significant advance in breeding for hardiness. Completely fertile with modern hybrid teas and floribundas, *Rosa kordesii* has spawned a series of shrub and climbing roses that are hardier than the average hybrid tea. Working with *Rosa kordesii*, *Rosa rugosa*, and various modern roses, Felicitas Svejda of Ontario has produced shrubs and climbers that can endure Canadian winters with little protection. And in Iowa, Griffith Buck has bred for hardiness using old species hybrids from Kordes, the central Asian *Rosa laxa*, and several modern grandifloras; many of these hybrids approach the individual floral beauty of modern floribundas and hybrid teas.

With geneticists and knowledgeable hybridizers working toward the "ultimate" rose—one that combines beauty with foolproof performance—we can expect roses to improve more rapidly in the coming years than they did in the past, when rosarians sowed naturally set seeds and hoped for exciting differences.

A Few Rose Terms to Know

As you read about roses, you're bound to run across certain terms again and again. Here are a few of the most frequently used words and phrases in the rose-growing world.

Bud. In rose jargon, this word has several meanings. First, of course, it refers to an unopened flower. It may also refer to the growth bud or growth "eye" found where leaves join stems. And *budding* is a common propagation technique: a plant is developed from a growth eye by a special grafting technique.

Bud union. On a commercially propagated rose bush, the bud union is the enlarged, knoblike part of the plant, generally 1 to 3 inches above the roots, where top growth joins with the understock. All major stems grow from the bud union, which increases in size each year.

Canes. The principal stems which grow from the bud union (or from very low on the bush) and form a rose's basic structure.

Code name. Many new roses are registered with the international rose registry under an offical code name; the roses may be sold, however, under one or more commercial "synonyms" that have greater popular appeal. The first three letters of the official code name generally incorporate part of the name of the originator or introducing firm, e.g. Mac- for McGredy, Mei- for Meilland. In the case of 'Bonica '82', described on page 56, the commercial name is given first; the code name is 'Meidomonac'.

Double. In some 19th-century rose literature, a double flower is defined as containing 10 to 14 petals—that is, about twice the number of petals that a single flower possesses. Today, a double flower is considered to be one containing 25 petals or more; very full-petaled flowers are called "very double."

Growth eye. An undeveloped growth bud that can produce a new lateral. The eye is a small bump on a stem immediately above the point where a leaf is attached (or where a leaf was once attached). In the photo of 'Olympiad' (page 16), a growth eye is visible where the topmost leaf joins the stem of the upper blossom.

Hip. If a rose is pollinated (as frequently happens naturally), a seed pod—the *hip*—can form after the flower's petals fall. Rose hips often turn brilliant colors in autumn.

Lateral. A secondary stem that arises from a growth eye along a main cane.

Rose Types At A Glance

Hybrid tea
The dominant rose class in modern rose gardens. The long, pointed buds and semi-double to double flowers are large and well formed. Plants are generally 3 to 5 feet tall.

Floribunda
Individual flowers are smaller than those of hybrid teas and are borne in clusters, producing a good mass display. Individual blooms may be single to double; some are informal in shape, others as shapely as hybrid teas. The bushy plants grow from 2 to 4 feet high.

Grandiflora
Descended from crosses between hybrid teas and floribundas, roses of this class combine hybrid tea beauty with the greater bloom production of the floribundas. Medium to large flowers usually come in small clusters on tall-growing (5- to 8-foot) plants.

Climber
Climbing roses have long, rather flexible canes that reach a considerable length—from 8 feet to 20 feet or more. They are typically grown against a wall or fence, though "pillar roses" can be trained upright. Some climbers are sports of bush hybrid teas, grandifloras, or floribundas; others are called "large-flowered climbers."

Pegging down. The practice of bending and securing to the ground canes of certain roses (hybrid perpetuals, various shrub roses) that have arching or lax growth. Flowering laterals will then grow along the bent-over canes.

Pillar rose. A relatively small-growing climbing rose that can be trained upright and still produce flowering laterals from buds along the canes.

Plant patent. Most new rose introductions are patented. This means that, during the 17-year period when the patent is in force, the patent holder and the rose's originator receive a small percentage from the sale of each plant. A patent provides a strong guarantee that plants you purchase will be well-grown and true to name. It also stimulates research and hybridizing, since the hybridizer is assured of some financial reward for his work.

Semidouble. A semidouble rose flower contains roughly between 8 and 20 petals, arranged in more than one layer but still opening to show stamens in the blossom center.

Single. A rose flower that consists of five to eight petals is said to be *single*. The petals are arranged in one layer around a single boss of stamens.

Sport. A change in growth habit or flower color that may occur suddenly on an established variety. A climbing form of a bush variety typifies a growth sport; 'Chicago Peace', a pink and orange blend, is an example of a color sport found on a plant of the normally light yellow and pink 'Peace'.

Stamens. The pollen-bearing parts of a flower, grouped in the flower's center. Each stamen consists of an *anther* (which contains the pollen) at the end of a thread-like filament.

Standard. Commonly called a "tree rose," a *standard* is just a bush rose budded high on an understock stem. Sizes vary greatly—from miniature standards on foot-tall stems to 2-foot patio standards, 3-foot regular standards, and even 6-foot weeping standards featuring flexible-caned ramblers.

Sucker. Any growth that arises from below the bud union on a budded plant. This growth is that of the understock and should be removed (see page 87).

Understock. The rose that furnished the root system to plants propagated by budding (see pages 92-93).

Standard or "Tree" rose
A product of the propagator's art, this is a bush rose budded onto an understock stem to produce a rose "tree." Miniature standards are budded on short (1- to 2-foot) stems; floribundas, hybrid teas, and grandifloras are typically budded onto 2- to 3-foot stems.

Shrub rose
This is a cover term used to describe a diverse group of mixed-ancestry roses that do not fit any of the established classifications. Flower sizes vary from small to large, plants from 4 to 10 feet tall; all are noted for performing well as flowering shrubs in the landscape.

Old garden rose
The various classes of roses that came into existence before the hybrid teas emerged in 1867 are collectively referred to as "old garden roses." Included are the favorites of years gone by, many with "old-fashioned" shape and notable fragrance. Refer to pages 6 to 11 for descriptions of the principal classes.

Miniature rose
The modern miniature roses are derived from miniature China roses and hybrid teas, grandifloras, and floribundas. Flower size is in the 1- to 2-inch range, on plants generally 2 feet or less in height. Color range includes all the shades found in modern hybrid teas, in flowers that range from informal to hybrid tea style.

To many, the word "rose" brings just one
image to mind: a red, red rose like 'Olympiad', the 1984 AARS winner pictured here.
You'll find a description on page 32.

Roses
in Your
Landscape

In versatility, few other flowering ornamentals come close to matching the rose. Its use in the garden is really limited by only three factors: your garden's size, its suitability for roses in general, and your imagination.

Technically speaking, all roses are flowering shrubs. Yet members of the group vary widely, from miniatures under a foot tall to climbing sorts that consider a 50-foot tree no obstacle. Such variety yields a wealth of choices that can provide vibrant color from spring to frost (even year-round, in frost-free climates), offer an assortment of foliage textures and hues, even sparkle with autumn displays of bright fruit.

Joseph's Coat

The following pages touch upon the many effects you can achieve with roses—lavish sweeps of color, charming mixed borders, the bold statement made by a single carefully placed plant—in settings ranging from formally structured to nearly wild. "Designing with Roses," pages 18 to 23, illustrates a number of landscaping options involving both old garden and modern varieties. In "Where to Grow Roses" (page 24), you'll find an outline of the basic requirements and restrictions to keep in mind as you choose garden locations for your roses. For tips on spacing, color harmony, and garden design, turn to the "Layout" section on page 26.

Designing with Roses

Using different rose types and different landscaping styles, you can create a multitude of garden effects. Here, presented in both words and pictures, are some of the possibilities.

The "rose garden"

Perhaps the most familiar rose planting is the garden or garden area devoted exclusively to roses. This is the stronghold of the modern hybrid tea, its larger grandiflora cousins, and, to a lesser extent, the floribunda. Standard ("tree") roses are sometimes incorporated to vary the height of such a planting. The more formal of these gardens are laid out in rows of military precision, with each bed separated from the next by pathways of lawn or paving. This is an efficient layout for a cutting garden; it is also the plan most likely to fit the greatest number of plants into a given area while allowing adequate space for development and care.

If the design is relaxed a bit, by flowing curves or irregularly shaped beds, the effect becomes more informal. And to make the picture softer still, you can vary the types of roses and their placement—planting climbers, for example, then adding shrub types or species roses for punctuation among modern sorts. Miniatures, polyanthas, or low floribundas might border the area with a low ribbon of color.

A rose garden in the classic style features rectangular planting beds, pathways of manicured lawn, and—for vertical interest—latticework for climbing varieties.

Devotees of old garden roses have considerable variety to work with. A varied all-rose garden can be achieved by combining the different classes to provide interesting contrasts in plant habit, foliage color and texture, and flower color and form.

Cottage gardens & mixed borders

Created by factory and piecework laborers, the earliest cottage gardens were small-scale plantings that combined edible and ornamental plants in a random (and often riotous) array. As the cottage garden gained the status of an art form in Victorian and Edwardian England, its working-class origins were obscured—but it retained the

Formal planting schemes accommodate the most roses in a given space. Here, rigidity is avoided by curving the beds to repeat the pool's curved margin.

A rose enthusiast can always find room for one more. When perimeter planting space is filled, new plants can be set out in "islands" in the lawn.

essential variety of the original, with beds of roses and other flowering shrubs, diverse perennials and annuals, and the more decorative vegetables.

The modern "mixed border" represents an evolution of the cottage garden style, featuring roses of all sorts in company with a number of other flowering plants. Among the floribundas, miniatures, and old garden roses, you'll find countless choices for mixed borders; the miniature roses and low-growing floribundas can function as bedding plants that offer colorful bloom almost all year long.

Roses as shrubs

The rose's immense popularity as a cut flower tends to overshadow the fact that roses are really shrubs and, as such, can perform striking duty in the landscape. Use them as borders, hedges, backgrounds, specimen plants—in short, in virtually any role that other shrubs can play (windbreak plantings excepted).

You'll find good shrub choices in many classes. Among the modern roses, the best "shrubby" plants appear among the grandifloras, floribundas, and polyanthas. Even the larger-growing miniatures—if pruned lightly or not at all—can become full, shrubby, and beyond miniature in height and spread.

A number of the old garden roses are attractive both out-of-bloom and in flower—albas, gallicas, teas, Chinas, Portlands, and Bourbons in particular. Also available are numerous species of roses and mixed-ancestry hybrids that are strictly shrub roses; see pages 56 and 57 for descriptions. Most species and many of their first-generation hybrids flower in spring only, then show off bright

The contemporary mixed border features a variety of easy-to-grow annuals and perennials interspersed with a number of modern miniature roses.

A mixed border in the typical cottage garden style showcases old garden rose 'Baronne Prévost' along with campanulas, catmint, irises, and geraniums.

Roses predominate in this cottage garden assortment of shrubs, perennials, and annuals. Foreground shrub roses give way to a short border of miniatures, with climbing miniature 'Red Wand' as background focal point.

autumn foliage and decorative hips later in the year. The repeat-flowering rugosas and their hybrids offer flowers and colorful hips simultaneously. A number of the mixed-ancestry hybrids flower repeatedly throughout the growing season; among these are the hybrid musks, popular plants that flourish in partial shade as well as in sunny locations.

The accent plant

There's no denying the visual impact of a mass of roses in full flower. But a single plant, strategically placed, can create just as much of a stir. The absence of competing roses focuses attention on the beauty of the individual: a climbing rose smothering a pergola, covering a wall, or ascending a post; a large shrub rose in solitary splendor;

one carefully groomed standard at attention by the front door; a floribunda beside the mailbox. Even a pampered miniature in a container can elicit admiring exclamations.

The contained rose

Rose growing need not be limited to beds in the open ground. Using containers and raised beds, you can establish a rose garden on your patio, terrace, deck, or balcony. Miniatures, polyanthas, and floribundas are especially suited to container life; some of these are also sold as standards on 1½- to 2-foot stems, so you can grow seasonal annuals beneath them in the same container. Small containers can be moved to soak up seasonal sun or to avoid winter weather; miniatures can even thrive indoors, if temperature, humidity, and light are satisfactory.

The rose arbor is a classic garden entry that's old fashioned yet never out of date. Rambler 'American Pillar' furnishes lavish spring display of single carmine-pink blossoms.

You don't need an entire rose garden to make a colorful landscape statement. Here, just one well-grown hybrid tea provides plenty of visual impact.

Fragrance and floral beauty combine in 'Bojangles', a miniature tree rose that reaches a height of just 2 feet.

For close-up enjoyment on patio or deck, try planting roses in containers. Floribundas and miniatures are natural candidates for this treatment, as 'Pillow Talk' (floribunda) demonstrates here.

Where to Grow Roses

Growing good roses is not difficult (see pages 64 to 94), but you do need to keep a few basic principles in mind. Choosing the right location is the first step toward success, since roses do not like to be moved: transplanting becomes more difficult as years pass and size increases, and larger plants take longer to reestablish. By selecting congenial sites at the outset, you should be rewarded by years of increasing pleasure as your rose garden prospers.

Keep the following points in mind when you evaluate possible planting sites:

■ Roses flourish in sunny locations. Most types need at least 6 hours of sunshine daily, preferably in the morning. Where weather is consistently cool or frequently overcast, plant roses where they'll be in full sun all day. On the other hand, intense summer heat calls for shelter from bright, scorching afternoon sun; try to locate the rose garden where afternoon sun will be filtered through trees growing at some distance from the roses.

Some old garden roses, climbers, and shrub roses (particularly the hybrid musks) will thrive in partial or filtered shade. Do make sure that they receive adequate light, though: dense, oppressive shade will defeat even the shade-tolerant types.

■ Roses prefer an ample supply of water and nutrients, so you should choose companion and neighboring plantings carefully. Annuals and most perennials offer no serious competition, but some trees and shrubs have greedy, shallow root systems that will usurp the water and fertilizer meant for your roses. Be sure you know the nature of any shrubs and trees you intend to plant near your rose garden; likewise, investigate the characteristics of those already growing close to the proposed site.

■ Avoid planting roses in windswept places. Strong or continuous winds spoil flowers and cause rapid transpiration from leaves, forcing you to water more often than you normally would.

■ Roses prefer fast-draining yet moisture-retentive soil. If clay soil renders your garden swamplike, or if you have a sandy yard that drains like a sieve, be sure to read the information on soil preparation and improvement on pages 69 and 70. If a hardpan layer is the culprit, raised beds of wood or masonry provide a practical, good-looking solution. Buried drainage tiles or perforated pipes can help drain a gently sloped site.

■ If your garden is on a relatively steep slope, you'll probably need to terrace your plantings. Wooden railroad ties, concrete blocks, brick, or even stone (if you're ambitious and skillful) all make fine retaining walls for terraced beds. See page 71 for details.

As you contemplate planting locations, you should also consider two additional points. First, your enjoyment will be enhanced if you plant your roses where they will be visible from inside the house. Second, envision an expansion plan. Your success with roses is likely to whet your appetite for more—and each year brings new and unfamiliar kinds you'll want to try.

Bedecked with blooming climbers, a graceful archway beckons the stroller into the rose garden beyond.

A single rose variety set out in a precise geometrical pattern creates a formal, one-color rose garden that perfectly suits a formal setting.

Heavy-blooming 'Climbing Mrs. Sam McGredy' mantles a split-rail fence in color and scent. An old favorite, this variety is one of the best climbing hybrid tea sports.

Layout

With so many attractive varieties available, you may be tempted to buy every plant you find interesting, then crowd them all into one big, sunny bed. If you are in danger of succumbing to this temptation, *don't!* For best results, consider the layout guidelines below.

Easy-maintenance design

Because all roses will probably need some fertilizing, pruning, and occasional attention to pest control, it's well worthwhile to plan a layout that makes maintenance simple. Easiest to care for are beds narrow enough to let you reach the plants in the center from either side—that way, you can perform all routine tasks without walking through the roses and compacting the soil around them. Tending beds that abut a fence or wall is simpler if the planting is two, or at most three, bushes deep. If you set your roses out in parallel rows, you'll find that staggered spacing makes for easier maintenance.

A rose garden bordered by lawn will inevitably require edging, but you can do two things to make the job easier. First, keep the number of separate beds to a minimum; this cuts down on the number of feet of edges you'll have to trim. Second, a mowing strip of brick, concrete, or wood between lawn and bed will keep the bed edges even—and simplify mowing right up to them.

Spacing

How far apart you plant your roses depends on three factors: your climate, the particular roses you choose, and the type of planting—an all-rose garden or a mixed border of roses plus assorted shrubs, annuals, and perennials. In all cases, it's important to allow each plant adequate room to grow and develop, and to leave enough space between plants to make tending the garden easy.

Where winter cold forces you to prune down to 1 to 2 feet each spring (see pages 86 to 89) and the following growing season is short, rose bushes seldom achieve the bulk they do in warmer regions. Planted 2 to 2½ feet apart, hybrid teas and grandifloras will fill in the bed without becoming tangled. In warmer areas—most of the South, Southwest, and West—hybrid teas and grandifloras should normally go about 3 feet apart. And where there is little or no frost to bring on definite winter dormancy (as in Florida, the Gulf Coast region, and parts of Southern California and the Southwest), roses grow so prodigiously all year that they need to be planted 4 feet or more apart.

Floribundas and polyanthas are generally smaller but bushier than hybrid teas and grandifloras, and are often massed for group effect. Except for especially vigorous, spreading varieties, space them about 2 feet apart in colder climates, 2½ feet apart where winters are relatively mild.

Despite the class name, miniature roses include varieties that, in mild climates, can reach up to 3 feet high and wide if not restrained by pruning. For mass effect (such as border plantings), set the smaller miniatures about 1 foot apart; give the larger sorts about double that distance.

Standard roses make available all the popular modern rose classes—hybrid teas, grandifloras, floribundas, polyanthas, and miniatures—budded onto stems 1 to 3 feet tall, depending on the plant's ultimate size. Since you plant these roses for their accent value, you want to be sure that the mature head—as it will grow in your climate—won't be crowded by its neighbors. If you plant your standards in a row, set them farther apart than you would space regular bushes of the same class.

Most shrub roses and many old garden types need more elbow room than modern hybrids, but just how much depends upon the growth habits of the particular varieties or species. As a general rule, allow from 5 to 6 feet between plants, perhaps a little more for any bushes whose canes you plan to peg down to get bloom all along their length.

Color harmony

Some gardeners feel that all nature's colors combine pleasantly. But if the idea of a screaming orange 'Tropicana' next to the deep, cold pink of 'Miss All-American Beauty' makes you grit your teeth, then you'll want to give some thought to establishing a good-neighbor color policy in your rose bed.

Colors that need the greatest care in placement are the pure, unshaded tones: clear orange and orange scarlet, bright red, deep yellow, and dark pink. The even orange of 'Tropicana' is more difficult to harmonize than the blended orange-copper of 'Mojave', for example—'Tropicana', being entirely one shade, almost always contrasts with its neighbors, whereas a yellow blend may pick up some of the paler orange tones of 'Mojave' and tie the two together. It's true that dazzling contrasts can be established by placing pure, bright colors side by side (such as yellow next to red or orange), but too much of this assaults the eye rather than pleases it. White roses are a safer bet for good-looking contrast with clear, vivid shades.

The easiest colors to mix throughout your rose plantings are cream, buff, light yellow, yellow blends, pink blends, and yellow and pink combinations. These tones all act as buffers for the strong hues and help tie unrelated colors together. For example, a soft yellow and pink 'Peace' planted between magenta and orange varieties will prevent an otherwise violent clash. Lavender and mauve roses associate nicely with the soft and blended colors, as well as with the dark, rich reds and most deep yellows. The ultimate "safe" color scheme is monochromatic: the "white garden," for example.

Appropriate growth habit

Beyond being compatible in color, the roses you choose must suit each other—and the garden space—in size and growth habit. A rampant 30-foot climber will be entirely unsuited to a 10-foot-wide patio wall, for example, whereas a climber of moderate growth (or even a lax-growing shrub) would fit the landscape admirably. Similarly, don't put a modest little bush like 'Angel Face' behind a robust giant like 'Queen Elizabeth'; you'll never see it.

Thanks to mass planting of floribunda-shrub 'Simplicity', this patio enclosure is colorful throughout the growing season.

Broad border planting offers a riot of color from spring through autumn. Modern hybrid teas mingle with floribundas and climbers; prominent white rose is shrubby floribunda 'Iceberg'.

Public rose gardens offer the prospective grower a great opportunity to view numerous varieties and rate their perform- ance. Here, floribunda 'City of Belfast' shows its colors in Portland.

A Shopper's Guide to Roses

Old Blush

From the rose varieties described in this chapter, you'll be able to make some preliminary choices for your garden. The first 26 pages cover the popular modern roses; the rest of the section highlights species, shrub roses, and old garden types.

Because color is usually the first deciding factor in choosing a rose, we have grouped all our modern roses (except climbers) by predominant color. As one might expect, though, not all roses accept easy categorization. Red, for example, runs from blackish crimson to scarlet-orange; white includes ivory and blush roses too pale to qualify as yellow or pink. Perhaps the greatest challenge lies in separating pink, orange, and multicolor. To confound matters further,

the degree of orangeness or pinkness can vary with the weather. We have simply classed as "multicolor" all roses exhibiting a combination of orange or pink plus one or more other distinct colors.

So much depends on climate, pruning, and general culture that it's impossible to give an absolute height for each rose described. Nonetheless, the relative sizes of low, medium, and tall will apply no matter where a particular rose is grown.

For all roses except miniatures and species, we list the year the rose was introduced to commerce. A designation of AARS means that the rose received the All-America Rose Selections award (see page 62).

Chrysler Imperial   *Christian Dior*   *Europeana*

Red Roses

NAME & TYPE	COLOR	DESCRIPTION
American Pride Hybrid Tea 1974	Rich red	Deep red, ovoid buds unfurl to full, lightly fragrant blossoms; recurved petal edges give each petal a pointed tip, resulting in a flower with a starlike look. Glossy medium green foliage; moderate plant height.
American Spirit Hybrid Tea 1988	Bright red	Long, pointed dark red buds open to large, full blossoms of unchanging bright red, with petals that appear cut from velvet. Flowers are equally good in warm or cool climates. Tall plant with dark, glossy foliage.
Christian Dior Hybrid Tea 1958 *Photo above*	Cherry-red	AARS 1962. Elegant blood-red buds unfurl to unscented blooms of a slightly lighter red, a bit lighter and duller on outsides of petals than on insides. Flowers remain attractive when fully open and do not fade or turn bluish. Tall plant.
Chrysler Imperial* Hybrid Tea 1952 *Photo above*	Dark crimson	AARS 1953. Classic, velvety dark red with shapely buds, full flowers, and rich fragrance; blossoms become purplish red as they age. Bushy, free-flowering plants of medium height have dark green, rather dull foliage.
City of Belfast Floribunda 1968 *Photo page 28*	Orange-red	Clusters of plump buds open to full, ruffled, moderate-size flowers of blazing orange-red. Plants are low and mounded, with glossy bronze-tinted leaves. Reliably profuse bloom in both warm and cool regions.
Crimson Glory* Hybrid Tea 1935	Dark crimson	Until the arrival of its offspring 'Chrysler Imperial', this was *the* red rose. Lovely buds open to full, velvety dark red flowers with a powerful fragrance. A vigorous plant with a low, spreading habit; not at its best in cool climates.
Dolly Parton Hybrid Tea 1984 *Photo page 31*	Orange-red	Both the large, pointed-ovoid buds and full, intensely fragrant blossoms are glowing orange-red. Medium-tall, spreading bushes have large, dark leaves that are somewhat susceptible to mildew.
Europeana Floribunda 1963 *Photo above*	Ruby-red	AARS 1968. Low, spreading, strong-growing bushes produce very large clusters of blooms in unfading bright, deep red. Individual flowers are full and rosette shaped, up to 3 inches across.

*Also available as a climber.

Mikado

Grand Masterpiece

Impatient

Dolly Parton

NAME & TYPE	COLOR	DESCRIPTION
Garnette Floribunda 1951	Dark crimson	Originally used chiefly as a florist's rose. The very full, rosette-shaped, dark crimson blossoms last 7 to 10 days as cut flowers, and open blooms never lose their attractiveness. Hollylike foliage is subject to mildew.
Grand Masterpiece Hybrid Tea 1978 *Photo above*	Bright red	A bright red, long-stemmed rose with classic features. Long, pointed buds unfurl to full blossoms of bright, rich, unfading red with light fragrance. Plant is tall and especially vigorous.
Gypsy Hybrid Tea 1972	Orange-red	AARS 1973. Blackish-red buds open to full ember-red flowers that seem to glow from within. The vigorous, medium-tall bushes bear dark bronzy green, disease-resistant foliage.
Impatient Floribunda 1984 *Photo above*	Orange-red	AARS 1984. Is it red or is it orange? Vivid orange-scarlet buds, freely produced on upright plants, open to 3-inch blossoms in a softer shade. Mahogany-hued new growth, compatible to the flower color, matures to glossy dark green.
Interama Floribunda 1976	Bright red	Brilliant color—and plenty of it—comes from clustered, moderately full flowers that resemble small hybrid teas. Bushy, free-branching plants have dark green, disease-resistant foliage.
Jennifer Hart Hybrid Tea 1982	Deep red	Carried on long stems, the pointed-ovoid buds open to velvety dark red blossoms full of petals and moderately fragrant. Plants are vigorous, medium-size to tall, with disease-resistant, semiglossy foliage.
Love Grandiflora 1980	Red and white	AARS 1980. Brilliant red petals with silvery white backs unfold from beautifully pointed buds; half-open blooms are a combination of red and white, while the fully opened blossoms appear totally red. Somewhat spreading; medium height.
Mikado Hybrid Tea 1988 *Photo above*	Cherry-red	AARS 1988. Bright cherry-red, accented with a touch of yellow at petal bases. Urn-shaped, flat-topped buds unfold to full, unfading blossoms with a light fragrance. Medium-size plant, covered with highly glossy leaves.

Mister Lincoln   *Showbiz*

...Red Roses

NAME & TYPE	COLOR	DESCRIPTION
Mirandy Hybrid Tea 1945	Dark red	AARS 1945. Full, intensely fragrant flowers of velvety dark red open from plump, pointed-ovoid buds. Performance is outstanding in warm, humid regions, but blooms tend to "ball" and turn purple in cool, foggy areas. Very bushy plant.
Mister Lincoln Hybrid Tea 1964 *Photo above*	Rich red	AARS 1965. A completely satisfactory and satisfying rich red for all regions. Long, lovely buds open to very full, long-stemmed flowers with a powerful fragrance. Tall, strong-growing plant; dark, glossy foliage.
Oklahoma* Hybrid Tea 1964 *Photo page 33*	Black-red	The blackest buds imaginable open to very large, rather globular, dusky red blooms that remain beautiful when fully open. Intensely fragrant. Plant is a lusty grower, but flowers are not at their best in cool, foggy regions.
Old Smoothie Hybrid Tea 1970	Rich red	Classic large, rich red, high-centered blooms on long stems are borne on a tall, slightly spreading plant. This rose's name refers to its lack of thorns: some stems are entirely thornless, while others have just a few prickles.
Olé* Grandiflora 1964 *Photo page 33*	Red-orange	Very full, ruffled and frilled blooms of blinding red-orange could almost be mistaken for tuberous begonias or oversize carnations. Bushy, vigorous, medium-height plants have dark hollylike leaves.
Olympiad Hybrid Tea 1984 *Photo page 16*	Bright red	AARS 1984. Tall, upright plant produces brilliant bright red blossoms on cutting-length stems. Long buds open to large, long-lasting, lightly scented flowers that hold their color without turning bluish. Dark, healthy foliage.
Precious Platinum Hybrid Tea 1974	Rich red	Practically a foolproof rose, this healthy, husky, medium-tall bush bears quantities of fragrant, medium-size, long-lasting blooms in unfading rich crimson. Glossy, disease-resistant foliage.
Proud Land Hybrid Tea 1969	Bright red	Heavy, penetrating fragrance emanates from full-petaled, velvety bright red blossoms. Buds are long, pointed, and freely produced on long stems. Plant is of medium height, vigorous and upright.
Razzle Dazzle Floribunda 1977	Red and white	Snappy color combination—red petals with white backs—inspired this rose's name. Petal edges of tapered buds scroll back, emphasizing the contrast. Flowers are moderately full, lightly scented; plant grows to medium height.
Red Devil Hybrid Tea 1970	Bright, light red	Long, lovely buds on long stems open to full, symmetrical flowers; the unfading red petals have lighter, almost silvery reverses. Upright plant of medium height with handsome, glossy foliage.

*Also available as a climber.

Oklahoma   Snowfire   Olé

NAME & TYPE	COLOR	DESCRIPTION
Red Lion Hybrid Tea 1964	Cherry-red	Large, moderately full flowers open so slowly that they turn in a good show in both cool and warm regions. Both the long, shapely buds and the open flowers are a bright, light cherry-red, carried on a tall, upright bush with large, dark leaves.
Red Masterpiece Hybrid Tea 1974	Dark red	Where days are sunny and warm, this dark red will provide plenty of pointed-ovoid buds that open to velvety, intensely fragrant, full flowers that take on black shadings as they mature. Tall, strong-growing plant.
Royal Velvet Hybrid Tea 1986	Bright red	Jaunty, wavy-petaled, moderately full flowers of bright, unfading red develop from dark red, pointed-ovoid buds on good cutting stems. Lightly scented. Medium-tall bush boasts attractive dark, leathery foliage.
Sarabande Floribunda 1957 *Photo page 64*	Oriental red	AARS 1960. Neon-bright Oriental red flowers are nearly single, showing decorative clusters of yellow stamens. Vigorous, low, spreading plants bloom continuously, are good for foreground plantings and hedges.
Scarlet Knight Grandiflora 1966	Scarlet	AARS 1968. Plump black-red buds in small clusters unfurl to velvety bright, thick-petaled blooms to 5 inches across. Bushy, thorny, vigorous plants grow to medium height; bear dark bronze-green foliage.
Showbiz Floribunda 1981 *Photo page 32*	Scarlet	AARS 1985. A first-rate landscape shrub, offering nearly continuous bloom on a robust, almost disease-proof plant. Long-lasting, intense scarlet flowers are semi-double with ruffled petals.
Snowfire Hybrid Tea 1970 *Photo above*	Red and white	The name describes the colors: brilliant, velvety red petals with white backs. Ovoid buds open to lightly fragrant, average-size blossoms. Upright, thorny plants of medium height bear handsome, glossy dark green leaves.
Toro (Uncle Joe) Hybrid Tea 1971	Dark red	"Big" is the word for this robust dark red. Long, pointed-ovoid buds open slowly to very full, large, shapely blossoms atop long stems clothed in dark, leathery leaves. Moderately fragrant. Bush is tall and upright.
Trumpeter Floribunda 1977	Orange-red	Intense, blazing color—somewhere between orange and red—in very full, ruffled blossoms. The flowers, large for a floribunda, come singly or in small clusters. Bushy, glossy-leafed plant of low to medium height.
Viva Floribunda 1974	Clear red	In flower size and plant habit, this falls between a floribunda and hybrid tea. Shapely, clear red, 3-inch flowers come on cutting-length stems in few-flowered clusters. Medium-tall plant with glossy foliage.

Electron　　　　　　　*First Prize*　　　　　　　*Friendship*

Pink Roses

NAME & TYPE	COLOR	DESCRIPTION
Aquarius Grandiflora 1971	Cool pink	AARS 1971. Long, beautifully tapered buds flare open to full, stiff, lightly scented blossoms in cool pink overlaid with deeper rose toward the petal margins. Bush is tall and slender, with leathery foliage.
Betty Prior Floribunda 1935	Deep rose	All the charm of a wild rose and much of the vigor, too. Red buds open to rose-pink single blooms that resemble dogwood blossoms in size and shape. Free-blooming, strong-growing bush is tall and spreading; good hedge or shrub.
Bewitched Hybrid Tea 1967 *Photo page 35*	Medium rose	AARS 1967. Long, stylish-looking buds on long, strong stems open slowly to fragrant "show rose" flowers in rose-pink, with paler petal backs. Healthy gray-green foliage clothes the tall, compact plant.
Camelot Grandiflora 1964	Coral-pink	AARS 1965. Medium-size coral-pink blossoms, very full and fragrant, open from ovoid buds that usually come in clusters. Productivity and general health are note-worthy; tall, slightly spreading plants have near disease-proof foliage.
Cécile Brunner* Polyantha 1881	Light pink	Perfect miniature replicas of hybrid tea flowers come throughout the year in graceful, thin-stemmed clusters. If given little pruning, the bush will grow in time to a rounded medium height. Disease-resistant foliage.
Century Two Hybrid Tea 1971	Deep rose	This bears the "ideal" rosebud: large, long, full-petaled, and fragrant. Dark rose is the color, but the petals are slightly deeper in color on the backs. Husky, medium-tall, slightly spreading bush.
Charlotte Armstrong* Hybrid Tea 1940	Deep red-pink	AARS 1941. An old favorite, noted for its long, elegantly slim reddish-pink buds that open to full, fragrant, informal flowers of warm dark pink. Prolific bush; vigorous, medium-tall, and somewhat spreading.
Cherish Floribunda 1980	Coral-pink	AARS 1980. Floribunda in growth and bloom habit, but flowers are of hybrid tea size and shape. Soft coral-pink, urn-shaped buds spiral open to blossoms with rolled-back petal edges. Spreading bush of medium height; dark, glossy foliage.
China Doll* Polyantha 1946	Rose-pink	Very full, 1- to 2-inch flowers in rounded clusters may be produced so abundantly that they nearly obscure the glossy bright green foliage. Plants are low growing—about 1½ feet tall—and nearly thornless.

*Also available as a climber.

Bewitched

Headliner

Miss All-American Beauty

NAME & TYPE	COLOR	DESCRIPTION
Color Magic Hybrid Tea 1978	Pink blend	AARS 1978. The magic is in the change of colors: creamy pink buds open to large, fragrant, ivory-centered flowers that take on increasing infusions of deep reddish pink. Medium-tall, upright bush has unusually large leaves.
Confidence Hybrid Tea 1951	Pink blend	Pastel shades of pink, peach, yellow, and cream mingle in large, full, fragrant blossoms that open from plump, shapely buds. Flowers are best where days and nights are warm. Husky, bushy plant of medium height.
Dainty Bess* Hybrid Tea 1925	Rose-pink	Perfect single blossoms of delicate rose-pink are centered with contrasting maroon-red stamens. Most of the graceful 3- to 4-inch, five-petaled blooms come in small clusters on upright, medium tall bushes.
Duet Hybrid Tea 1960	Dusky pink	AARS 1961. Medium-size buds and blooms are very long lasting and lightly fragrant. Color is a two-tone dusky pink, with the darker shade on the petal backs. A terrific bloomer; medium-tall, with dark, hollylike foliage.
Electron Hybrid Tea 1970 *Photo page 34*	Deep pink	AARS 1973. Full-petaled, glowing hot pink blossoms slowly unfold from plump, shapely buds and hold their attractive shape well after opening. Upright medium height bush is clothed with especially handsome, disease-proof, glossy leaves.
Fashion Floribunda 1949	Coral-pink	AARS 1950. The first of the coral-colored floribundas and still an exquisite flower. Ovoid buds in small clusters open to fragrant, rather cup-shaped blooms about 3 inches across. Medium-low, bushy plant with bronzy foliage.
First Prize* Hybrid Tea 1970 *Photo page 34*	Rich pink	AARS 1970. Fabulous, very long, spiral buds of deep pink unfold to really large flowers that are distinctly lighter in the centers. Vigorous, medium-size, spreading bushes; dark foliage is somewhat susceptible to mildew.
Fragrant Memory **(Jadis)** Hybrid Tea 1974	Rose-pink	Powerful fragrance and beautiful form are the hallmarks of this heavy-blooming, clear pink rose. Slender, urn-shaped buds produce moderately full flowers in an intense, even color. Tall, slender plant.
Friendship Hybrid Tea 1978 *Photo page 34*	Salmon-pink	AARS 1979. Color varies from pink through coral and salmon shades, but the full blossoms are always long budded, shapely, and highly fragrant, carried on good cutting stems. Tall, upright bush has large, dark leaves.

*Also available as a climber.

Perfume Delight　　　　　　*Queen Elizabeth*　　　　　　*Seashell*

...Pink Roses

NAME & TYPE	COLOR	DESCRIPTION
Gene Boerner Floribunda 1968	Rose-pink	AARS 1969. In every detail, the buds and full blossoms are perfect scaled-down models of the best hybrid teas. Lightly fragrant flowers in an even rose-pink shade come both singly and in clusters on a medium-tall, upright plant.
Headliner Hybrid Tea 1985 *Photo page 35*	Pink-white blend	A lively pink and white combination that begins with long, graceful buds of creamy white brushed pink from petal edges; these spiral open to very full, dark cherry-pink flowers with glowing white centers. Tall bush.
Helen Traubel Hybrid Tea 1951	Salmon-pink	AARS 1952. Big, billowing bushes take up more space than many other hybrid teas but are well worth it for the great quantities of flowers they bear. Long, pointed salmon-apricot buds open quickly to large, rather loose flowers.
Michèle Meilland Hybrid Tea 1945	Creamy pink	Each beautifully tapered, slender bud opens to a medium-size perfect flower, varying in color from creamy pink to creamy amber. Bushy, rounded plant blooms profusely, reaches medium height.
Milestone Hybrid Tea 1985 *Photo page 2*	Coral-pink	Ovoid rose-red buds open to full, coral-pink flowers with lighter centers; as flowers age, petals gradually darken to coral-red. Medium-tall bush bears plenty of flowers against a backdrop of glossy foliage.
Miss All-American Beauty Hybrid Tea 1965 *Photo page 35*	Cerise	AARS 1968. A big, bold blossom in a color you can't overlook: something between a deep "shocking" pink and light red. Ovoid buds and very full, well-formed flowers come on a leathery-leafed, husky plant of medium height.
Mon Cheri Hybrid Tea 1981 *Photo page 37*	Pink to red	AARS 1982. The combination of vivid pink and glowing red is almost too bright to look at. Soft pink buds open out and become velvety red wherever the sun strikes the petals. Very full blossoms on a dark-foliaged bush of medium height.
Perfume Delight Hybrid Tea 1973 *Photo above*	Deep pink	AARS 1974. Rich, spicy fragrance is one asset; another is the flawless long, spiraled bud form. Buds unfurl to perfect 5-inch blooms of satiny deep pink. Medium-height plants are compact and upright, with large, dark leaves.
Pink Peace Hybrid Tea 1959	Deep rose	Not really a pink duplicate of 'Peace', yet it too produces numerous large, full, shapely blooms from plump, ovoid buds. Intense deep pink flowers have a heavy fragrance. Medium-height, upright bush, with foliage that is susceptible to rust.

Mon Cheri

Sonia

Royal Highness

NAME & TYPE	COLOR	DESCRIPTION
Prima Donna Grandiflora 1983	Raspberry-pink	AARS 1988. An even, cold, raspberry-sherbet pink. Long, very slender buds on long stems unfurl to well-shaped, moderately full blooms. Vigorous bush is tall and upright, with semiglossy leaves.
Promise Hybrid Tea 1976	Light pink	Clear, pure light pink color holds from the pointed-ovoid bud stage until the petals fall from the large, full, lightly fragrant blossoms. Tall, vigorous bush features glossy foliage of a rather light green.
Queen Elizabeth* Grandiflora 1954 *Photo page 36*	Clear pink	AARS 1955. For all practical purposes a shrub rose, suitable for hedges and background planting. Radiant pink, medium-size blooms develop from compact, pointed buds in small clusters. Tall and extremely vigorous, with glossy leaves.
Royal Highness Hybrid Tea 1962 *Photo above*	Blush-pink	AARS 1963. Porcelainlike blush-pink buds and flowers are of the highest quality. Long, pointed buds slowly unfold to magnificent full, sweetly fragrant blossoms. Upright, medium-tall plant has dark, glossy foliage.
Sea Pearl Floribunda 1964	Pink-cream blend	Long, shapely buds (large for a floribunda) borne on cutting-length stems combine peach to salmon tones with creamy yellow, the depth of color varying according to weather. Medium-tall bush with dark, leathery leaves.
Seashell Hybrid Tea 1976 *Photo page 36*	Salmon-pink	AARS 1976. Deep apricot buds unfold to full, fragrant blossoms in rich colors of salmon-pink to light orange, all with yellow tints. Dark green foliage clothes the medium-height, heavy-flowering bush.
Sheer Bliss Hybrid Tea 1987 *Photo page 4*	Pink and white	AARS 1987. Just barely pink—long, ovoid buds of a luscious creamy white lightly blushed pink open to full, fragrant flowers that are darker in the centers. Dark, glossy foliage on an upright plant of medium height.
Sonia Grandiflora 1974 *Photo above*	Coral-pink	Originally a greenhouse rose that "escaped" to the garden. Noted for its perfectly formed medium-size buds and fragrant, long-lasting, full and shapely open flowers of soft to deep coral-pink. Upright, medium-tall bush; dark foliage.
South Seas Hybrid Tea 1962	Coral-salmon	Open, gracefully ruffled, fragrant flowers are magnificent—really large and full, opening slowly from long buds of warm deep pink. Medium-tall, slightly spreading plant with bronzy leaves.

*Also available as a climber.

Tiffany

Tournament of Roses

...Pink Roses

NAME & TYPE	COLOR	DESCRIPTION
Summer Dream Hybrid Tea 1987	Pink blend	Colors of summer fruits—peach, melon, apricot—mingle in a large, full, beautifully formed flower that develops from long, ovoid, yellow-tinted buds. Dark, glossy foliage is displayed on an upright, medium-tall bush.
Sunrise-Sunset Hybrid Tea 1971	Pink-cream blend	The general pink effect stems from an artful blending of cream with sunset-pink shades. Large, shapely buds open to full flowers; the outer petals are strongly blushed pink, while the centers may be creamy lavender. Bush is tall and upright.
Sweet Surrender Hybrid Tea 1983 *Photo page 62*	Silvery pink	AARS 1983. Its heady perfume gave this rose its name. The pointed buds on long stems unfold to very full, large, silvery pink blossoms of old-rose charm. Upright bush of medium height.
The Fairy Polyantha 1932	Pale pink	Small flowers are of no special individual beauty, but they're produced in such quantity that the plant has great garden value. Pyramidal clusters of pale pink blooms are carried on medium-low, spreading bushes with glossy, disease-proof leaves.
Tiffany* Hybrid Tea 1954 *Photo above*	Warm pink	AARS 1955. Large, long buds, as perfect as finely cut jewels, open to moderately full, warm pink blossoms with an intense, fruity fragrance. Tall, upright plants have matte dark green foliage.
Touch of Class Hybrid Tea 1984 *Photo on front cover*	Warm pink	AARS 1986. Heavy-petaled, long-lasting blooms shade from coral and cream into a vibrant warm pink. Large, moderately full, lightly fragrant flowers open from tapered buds. The tall, upright bush is clothed in dark, glossy leaves.
Tournament of Roses Grandiflora 1988 *Photo above*	Warm pink	AARS 1989. Ovoid buds and camellialike open flowers display two shades of pink: dark coral on the petal backs, warm light pink on the insides. Glossy-leafed plants of medium height are noted for profuse flower production.
Tribute Hybrid Tea 1983	Cherry-pink	Glowing with color as though lighted from within, 'Tribute' really stands out in the garden. Long, tapered buds that open to large, vivid cherry-pink blossoms are freely produced on tall plants with dark, glossy foliage.

*Also available as a climber.

Amber Queen

Brandy

Orange Roses

NAME & TYPE	COLOR	DESCRIPTION
Ambassador Hybrid Tea 1979	Bright orange	Urn-shaped buds of glowing dark orange washed with yellow slowly open to full, long-stemmed orange-apricot blooms that are lightly scented. Glossy dark green leaves clothe the tall, vigorous bush.
Amber Queen Floribunda 1984 *Photo above*	Amber-gold	AARS 1988. High marks for flowers, foliage, and habit. Clusters of plump buds open to full, ruffly, scented blossoms of amber to gold-apricot. Foliage is dark, bronze tinted, almost quilted, on a bushy, medium-low plant.
Apricot Nectar Floribunda 1965	Creamy apricot	AARS 1966. Luscious creamy apricot hybrid tea–type blossoms, each up to 4 inches across, are borne in large clusters. Heavy-blooming, spreading plant of medium height; dark green foliage.
Arizona Grandiflora 1975	Copper-orange	AARS 1975. Urn-shaped buds open to glowing gold-tinted orange flowers highlighted against leaves of dark, coppery green. Tall, extra-vigorous bush; good as a specimen shrub or, if planted in groups, as a tall hedge.
Bing Crosby Hybrid Tea 1980	Persimmon-orange	AARS 1981. "Persimmon" is the best description of this rose's glowing orange color. Buds of medium length open into very full, lightly fragrant blossoms. Plant is tall, upright and spreading, with dark, glossy leaves.
Brandy Hybrid Tea 1981 *Photo above*	Gold-apricot	AARS 1982. The glowing golden apricot color suggested the name. Unfurling from burnt orange buds, the large, broad-petaled, mildly fragrant flowers open well in all weather. Dark green leaves (bronzy when new) complement the blossoms.
Caramella Hybrid Tea 1986	Copper-apricot	Here, orange is approached from the lighter, more golden side. Full, ovoid coppery apricot buds unfurl to many-petaled, lighter-hued flowers washed with pink. Medium-tall, spreading bush has semiglossy foliage.
Cary Grant Hybrid Tea 1987	Orange-red blend	You know from the name that this is an elegant rose. Long, tapered buds are vivid reddish orange, washed yellow at the bases; large, full, shapely, fragrant flowers are orange with a red overlay. Upright, medium-tall plant.

Fragrant Cloud

Mojave

Las Vegas

...Orange Roses

NAME & TYPE	COLOR	DESCRIPTION
First Edition Floribunda 1976	Coral-orange	AARS 1977. Here are perfect hybrid tea–type flowers brought down to floribunda size; the coral-orange blossoms appear both singly and in clusters. Plant is low but quite spreading, with bright green, leathery leaves.
Fragrant Cloud Hybrid Tea 1963 *Photo above*	Coral-orange	Coral-orange, 30-petaled flowers with an intense and delightful fragrance develop from long, scarlet-orange buds. Bushy, profusely blooming plants of medium height are clothed in glossy dark green leaves.
Gingersnap Floribunda 1978	Mandarin orange	Ruffled petals of glowing orange are packed into very full flowers of nearly hybrid tea size, borne in clusters on a rounded, bushy plant of medium height. Deep bronze-purple new growth matures to dark green.
Just Joey Hybrid Tea 1972	Buff-orange	Colors are soft rather than assertive. From attractive buff-orange buds come moderately full, highly fragrant flowers that soften to apricot shades. Large, glossy leaves adorn a bushy, upright plant of medium height.
Las Vegas Hybrid Tea 1981 *Photo above*	Orange-gold blend	Brilliant color is the 'Las Vegas' trademark. Shapely, pointed buds yield medium-size flowers of vibrant red-orange, the petal backs golden yellow blending to orange. The medium-tall plant is clothed in glossy foliage.
Margo Koster* Polyantha 1931	Light orange	Nearly round buds are composed of many shell-like petals that open into small, cupped, light orange flowers that resemble ranunculus blossoms. Flowers come in large clusters on a low, twiggy plant bearing glossy light green foliage.
Marina Floribunda 1974	Coral-orange	AARS 1981. Dark, glossy foliage contrasts handsomely with the vibrant orange flowers. Shapely buds are borne both singly and in clusters; hybrid tea–type blooms are long-lasting, fragrant. Upright plant of medium height.
Medallion Hybrid Tea 1973 *Photo page 41*	Light buff-orange	AARS 1973. Everything about this rose is large, from the extra-long buds to the open flowers to the plant itself. Buff-apricot in bud, the licorice-scented blossoms take on pink tones as they open. Tall, spreading habit; dark foliage.
Mojave Hybrid Tea 1954 *Photo above*	Burnt orange	AARS 1954. Stylish burnt orange buds, veined in a darker shade, open to moderately double, light orange-apricot blooms. Vigorous, very slender bushes have dark red-brown stems and glossy deep green leaves.

*Also available as a climber.

Montezuma   Medallion   Prominent

NAME & TYPE	COLOR	DESCRIPTION
Montezuma Grandiflora 1955 *Photo above*	Coral-orange	Beautifully formed buds lighten as they open, turning from near-red to coral-salmon (or coral-orange in warm weather). Flowers are long-lasting on bush or when cut. Tall, robust, slightly spreading plants have leathery, disease-resistant foliage.
New Year Grandiflora 1982 *Photo page 4*	Orange-gold blend	AARS 1987. On the short side (medium height) for a grandiflora, but no less vigorous. Dark, glossy leaves provide a handsome backdrop for a profusion of bright gold-orange buds and well-formed softer orange blossoms.
Oldtimer Hybrid Tea 1969	Bronze-apricot	Very large, elegant blossoms with satiny-textured petals develop from long, stream-lined buds. Color is golden apricot with tints of bronze or copper. Tall, upright bush bears leathery, pointed leaves.
Prominent Grandiflora 1971 *Photo above*	Brilliant orange	AARS 1977. Long-lasting, neon-bright blossoms of pure, deep orange are impossible to overlook. Each petal's edge recurves, forming a pointed tip—and creating a starlike flower. Bushes are of medium height, with thick, glossy leaves.
Shreveport Grandiflora 1981	Salmon-orange	AARS 1982. Blending of orange, salmon, coral, and yellow gives overall impression of soft orange. Shapely buds and full, medium-size flowers come one to a stem on tall, strong-growing plants.
Spartan Floribunda 1955	Coral-orange	Well-formed burnt orange buds open to full, coral-orange flowers of old-fashioned appearance; clustered, richly fragrant blossoms are larger than those of the average floribunda. Bushy, glossy-leafed plant of medium height.
Sundowner Grandiflora 1978	Pure orange	AARS 1979. Tall, exuberantly vigorous bushes produce their highly fragrant, glowing orange blossoms in small clusters during summer, but just one per stem during the spring bloom period. Foliage tends to mildew late in the season.
Sunfire Floribunda 1974	Bright orange	Three-inch hybrid tea–type flowers, as vibrant in color as 'Tropicana', come in clusters—but on individual stems long enough for cutting. Plentiful light green foliage clothes the medium-tall plant.
Tropicana* Hybrid Tea 1960	Orange-salmon	AARS 1963. Forerunner of the contemporary fluorescent orange roses. Medium-size, pointed buds open to full, sweet-scented, rather cupped flowers. Tall, semispreading plant has matte green leaves susceptible to mildew.

*Also available as a climber.

Chicago Peace

Broadway

Granada

Multicolor Roses

NAME & TYPE	COLOR	DESCRIPTION
Antigua Hybrid Tea 1974	Pink-gold blend	Its combined and variable colors—pink, apricot, gold—make 'Antigua' difficult to fit into a precise color class. Pointed buds open to large, fragrant, moderately full flowers carried on tall plants with glossy foliage.
Broadway Hybrid Tea 1986 *Photo above*	Pink-yellow blend	AARS 1986. Urn-shaped buds are golden orange suffused with pink; as the flowers open, the pink tones increase and intensify at petal edges, while the gold shades lighten to yellow. Tall, strong plant has dark, leathery foliage.
Caribia Hybrid Tea 1972	Red and yellow	The jester of the rose garden, 'Caribia' has bright yellow petals irregularly streaked with brilliant red. Vigorous but low growing, with bronzy foliage that complements the flower color.
Cathedral Floribunda 1975	Apricot and orange blend	AARS 1976. Small clusters of well-formed buds open to ruffled blossoms of apricot with orange-red shadings; each flowering stem yields a perfect bouquet. Glossy copper-tinted foliage densely covers the low, compact plant.
Charisma Floribunda 1977	Yellow, orange, red blend	AARS 1978. Rounded, spreading plant of medium height flaunts small, very full, rosette-shaped blooms of brilliant golden yellow edged orange-red. As the flower ages, each petal is entirely suffused with red. Dark, very glossy leaves.
Cherry-Vanilla Grandiflora 1973	Yellow and pink blend	Flowers in an engaging, changeable blend of cream to yellow, with each petal infused from the edges with varying amounts of reddish pink. The lightly fragrant flowers are borne on vigorous, medium-tall plants with dark green foliage.
Chicago Peace Hybrid Tea 1962 *Photo above*	Pink and copper blend	A color sport of 'Peace' (see next page) which retains all the virtues of foliage, plant, and magnificent flower form, but offers blooms in a livelier color blend—bronzy yellow, deep pink, and copper.
Circus Floribunda 1956	Yellow and red blend	AARS 1956. Buds in the best hybrid tea style are yellow with red at the edges; as the blooms open, more red infuses the petals to give them buff and pink shadings. Low, spreading bush with glossy foliage.
Double Delight* Hybrid Tea 1977	Red, cream, and white blend	AARS 1977. Unmistakable blooms of camellialike form: creamy white with cherry red brushed on petal edges. The amount of red varies according to weather, and increases as flowers age. Spreading, glossy-leafed bush of medium height.

*Also available as a climber.

Voodoo

Peace

NAME & TYPE	COLOR	DESCRIPTION
Fascination Hybrid Tea 1982	Pink, cream, and gold blend	Artful combination of ivory, apricot, coral, and gold appears in large, full flowers that mimic peonies in size and form. Vigorous, upright, many-caned plant is clothed in semiglossy foliage.
Granada* Hybrid Tea 1963 *Photo page 42*	Red and yellow blend	AARS 1964. Nasturtium-red, light yellow, and pink blend together into notably fragrant, moderately full, long-lasting flowers that open from slender, shapely buds. Dark green, hollylike foliage on upright plant of medium height.
Matador Hybrid Tea 1972	Red, yellow bicolor	As flashy as the name implies, in colors that would stimulate even the laziest of bulls. Short, pointed buds open to long-lasting two-tone blossoms: orange-red on petal faces, yellow on the backs. Medium-size plant with dark leaves.
Peace* Hybrid Tea 1945 *Photo above*	Yellow and pink blend	AARS 1946. Full, ovoid buds of yellow touched with pink or red slowly unfold into glorious, extra-large blossoms with pink-rimmed yellow petals. Strong, spreading bush of medium height has large, glossy leaves.
Princesse de Monaco Hybrid Tea 1981	Cream and pink blend	Dainty pastel colors combine in a blossom that is large and full, yet graceful. Plump, creamy yellow buds with pinkish-red margins slowly open to ivory-petaled blooms with a wider edge of cherry-pink. Medium-low, upright bush.
Redgold Floribunda 1971	Gold and red blend	AARS 1971. Shapely golden yellow buds are edged in red; as the moderately full flowers open, the petals become more deeply suffused with red. Medium-size, upright bush sports glossy dark green leaves.
Summer Fashion Floribunda 1985	Pink and yellow blend	The combination of soft colors creates a confectionlike blossom. Short, ovoid buds are cream and yellow with a pink edge on outer petals; fragrant, creamy flowers show more pink as they age. Low, bushy plant with dark foliage.
Sutter's Gold* Hybrid Tea 1950	Yellow, orange, red blend	AARS 1950. Powerfully fragrant flowers opening from elegantly long, bronzy yellow buds show a blend of yellow, pink, orange, and red. Best in cool climates, where the moderately full blossoms open more slowly and color holds longer. Tall bush.
Voodoo Hybrid Tea 1986 *Photo above*	Orange, yellow, and pink blend	AARS 1986. Yellow-orange buds open to large, heavily perfumed flowers that soften to yellow and peach shades, then finally fade to pink. Tall, upright bush carries plenty of dark bronze-green, glossy foliage.

*Also available as a climber.

Sunsprite

Oregold

Summer Sunshine

Gold Medal

Yellow Roses

NAME & TYPE	COLOR	DESCRIPTION
Arlene Francis Hybrid Tea 1957	Golden yellow	Long, pointed buds of beautiful form open to large, moderately full, golden yellow flowers with a powerful fragrance. Medium-size bushes are somewhat spreading, mantled in glossy dark green leaves.
Eclipse Hybrid Tea 1935	Medium yellow	An old favorite, loved for its long, stylish buds—the moderately full open flowers, though plentifully produced, are not especially attractive. Very vigorous, upright bush; dark grayish-green leaves.
Gold Badge Floribunda 1978	Golden yellow	Brilliant, unfading flowers are large—similar to small hybrid tea blossoms—and borne in small sprays. Hollylike foliage of glossy dark green clothes a fairly low, spreading bush.
Golden Masterpiece Hybrid Tea 1954	Deep yellow	Long, large buds expand into some of the largest blooms among roses—and the full, fragrant flowers hold their color well. Strong-growing plant is upright and bushy, outfitted in dark, highly glossy foliage.
Goldilocks Floribunda 1945	Medium yellow	The first good yellow floribunda and still worthwhile, though it doesn't hold its color as well as more recent introductions. Short, deep yellow buds open to very full, fragrant, clustered flowers that fade to cream. Bushy, medium-low plant.
Gold Medal Grandiflora 1982 *Photo above*	Golden yellow	Great vigor and good health are among this rose's winning traits. Small clusters of long, ovoid, golden yellow buds, sometimes tinged with pink or orange, unfurl to large, full, fragrant blossoms. Plant is very tall and upright.
Houston Hybrid Tea 1980	Deep yellow	Clear, brilliant, unshaded and unfading color make 'Houston' a beacon in the garden. Pointed buds produce full, sweetly-scented flowers. Plant is medium tall with dark, leathery foliage.
Katherine Loker Floribunda 1978	Butter-yellow	Moderately full blossoms of best hybrid tea form and clear, unshaded yellow color come singly and in small clusters. Free-flowering plant of medium height is upright and bushy, clothed in semiglossy foliage.

Sun Flare *New Day* *King's Ransom*

NAME & TYPE	COLOR	DESCRIPTION
King's Ransom Hybrid Tea 1961 *Photo above*	Deep yellow	AARS 1962. Long, classically formed buds open to large, full flowers with an unfading chrome-yellow color and a pronounced sweet fragrance. Upright, medium-tall plant bears dark, glossy leaves.
Lemon Spice Hybrid Tea 1966	Soft yellow	The name describes both the light lemon yellow color and the intense spicy scent. The many long buds open quickly to full blossoms that are sometimes too heavy for the stems to hold upright. Tall, spreading bush.
New Day Hybrid Tea 1977 *Photo above*	Soft yellow	Classically long, tapered buds and clear, unshaded color make this spicy-scented, free-blooming yellow rose a favorite. Upright, fairly thorny plants of medium height are dressed in leathery gray-green foliage.
Oregold Hybrid Tea 1975 *Photo page 44*	Saffron-yellow	AARS 1975. A tawny tint adds extra richness to the basic deep golden yellow hue. Long, pointed buds open to full, shapely, lightly scented blossoms in a softer yellow. Dark, glossy leaves clothe an upright, medium-size bush.
Summer Sunshine* Hybrid Tea 1962 *Photo page 44*	Brilliant yellow	Both the beautifully chiseled buds and moderately full, lightly fragrant open blooms have the most brilliant pure yellow color imaginable. Free-flowering, upright plant reaches medium height. Glossy green leaves have a bronzy tint.
Sunbright Hybrid Tea 1984	Deep yellow	Long, urn-shaped dark yellow buds open to large, moderately full flowers that hold their color well. Tall, robust plant blooms almost all year, its bright blossoms backed by glossy dark green leaves.
Sun Flare Floribunda 1983 *Photo above*	Lemon-yellow	AARS 1983. Low, compact, bushy plants produce great quantities of shapely, fragrant, 3-inch blossoms in clusters of small to moderate size; the luminous lemon color is nearly unfading. Dense, extra-glossy foliage is bright green.
Sunsprite Floribunda 1977 *Photo page 44*	Bright yellow	Small clusters of ovoid buds produce fragrant, wavy-petaled, brilliant yellow flowers that retain their color until petals fall. Upright bush is clothed in semiglossy leaves, blooms prolifically. Medium height.

*Also available as a climber.

Pascali

Honor

French Lace

White Roses

NAME & TYPE	COLOR	DESCRIPTION
Canadian White Star Hybrid Tea 1980	Pure white	Large, full, sparkling white blooms unfurl from long, shapely buds; petal edges roll back so that each petal is pointed, giving the flower a starlike appearance. Tall, leathery-foliaged plant bears best blossoms in cool climates.
Class Act Floribunda 1988 *Photo page 47*	Lemon-white	AARS 1989. Prolific flower production and disease resistance recommend this heavily foliaged rose for mass planting. Medium-small, lemon-white buds quickly open to moderately double flowers with a light fragrance.
Evening Star Floribunda 1974	Pure white	Not quite a hybrid tea, but not a floribunda, either. Medium-size, full, lightly fragrant flowers come in small clusters—but on cutting-length stems. Bushes of medium height are clothed in dark, healthy foliage.
French Lace Floribunda 1981 *Photo above*	Creamy white	AARS 1982. Buff-ivory buds develop into apricot-centered creamy-white blossoms that are crammed with petals in the style of some old roses. Dark, glossy, nearly disease-proof foliage covers a medium-tall, bushy plant.
Garden Party Hybrid Tea 1959	Pinkish ivory	AARS 1960. Long, tapered ivory buds are tinted pink on petal edges, with the pink shading often increasing as buds open to beautiful, stiffly perfect, ruffled blooms. Spreading medium-size plant has matte foliage that is susceptible to mildew.
Honor Hybrid Tea 1980 *Photo above*	Pure white	AARS 1980. Long, pointed satiny white buds unfurl slowly to really large, long-lasting blossoms that are only moderately full. Tall, upright plant with leathery olive-green leaves.
Iceberg* Floribunda 1958 *Photo page 27*	Pure white	This tall, bushy plant is more like a shrub rose than a typical floribunda. Long, pointed buds open to sweet-scented flowers of nearly hybrid tea size. Light green, disease-proof foliage.
Ivory Tower Hybrid Tea 1979	Pinkish ivory	Marblelike, long but full buds unfold to full, fragrant, ivory-colored blooms with rolled petal edges; mature flowers may have subtle pink shading. Vigorous bush of medium height features dark, semiglossy foliage.
John F. Kennedy Hybrid Tea 1965	Pure white	Long, classically tapered buds, often green tinged, slowly spiral open to full, notably fragrant, pure white flowers of great size. Medium-tall plant has dark, leathery foliage; best bloom comes in warm regions.
Louisiana* Hybrid Tea 1969	Ivory-white	Large greenish-ivory buds on long stems slowly open to full, ivory-white blossoms that develop best in warm climates. Plant is especially tall and upright, with dark, leathery leaves.

*Also available as a climber.

Class Act

Pristine

Angel Face

NAME & TYPE	COLOR	DESCRIPTION
Pascali Hybrid Tea 1963 *Photo page 46*	Warm white	AARS 1969. More dependable in all climates than many other whites for perfectly formed medium-size buds and full, creamy white blossoms. Tall, upright plants with dark foliage are especially free flowering.
Pristine Hybrid Tea 1978 *Photo above*	Blush-white	Too pink to be really white, but too white to be classed with pinks. Long, ovoid, pink-blushed buds quickly open to full, long-lasting, pink-tinted ivory blooms with light fragrance. Medium-size bush has handsome, glossy leaves.
Saratoga Floribunda 1963	Pure white	AARS 1964. The emphasis is on performance. Vigorous, bushy, low, somewhat spreading plants continually produce clusters of fragrant, gardenialike blossoms against a backdrop of glossy bright green leaves.
White Lightnin' Grandiflora 1980	Creamy white	AARS 1981. Ruffled petals give the full, citrus-scented, creamy white blossoms a distinct personality. Bushy, free-flowering plants of medium height (short for a grandiflora) have bright, glossy leaves.
White Masterpiece Hybrid Tea 1969	Pure white	A masterpiece of classic form: long, ovoid buds open into very full, fragrant, really large blossoms. Recurved edges give each petal a pointed tip. Medium-tall, slightly spreading plant has glossy, disease-resistant foliage.

Lavender Roses

NAME & TYPE	COLOR	DESCRIPTION
Angel Face* Floribunda 1968 *Photo above*	Rosy lavender	AARS 1969. Ruffled, very full, very fragrant blooms, deep lavender enlivened by rose and red tints, are beautifully complemented by bronze-tinted deep green foliage. Low, spreading plant flowers heavily.
Blue Girl **(Kölner Karneval)** Hybrid Tea 1964	Silvery lavender	Shapely buds of silvery deep lilac open to full, cup-shaped flowers with a potent fragrance. Bushy, somewhat spreading plant grows to medium height, features dark, glossy foliage that is notably disease resistant.
Blue Nile Hybrid Tea 1981	Rich lavender	Moderately full blossoms in exotic rich lavender with darker shadings boast lovely form and heavy fragrance. Very vigorous, tall and slightly spreading plant bears large, bronze-tinted dark green leaves.

*Also available as a climber.

Heirloom

Paradise   *Lady X*   *Intrigue*

...Lavender Roses

NAME & TYPE	COLOR	DESCRIPTION
Deep Purple Floribunda 1980	Plum-purple	Despite the name, the usual flower color ranges from magenta to light plum. The ovoid buds develop into full, camellialike blossoms. Moderately fragrant. Dark, glossy foliage covers a plant of medium height.
Heirloom Hybrid Tea 1972 *Photo above*	Magenta blend	From ovoid, deep lilac to purple buds come full, deliciously fragrant flowers in rich lilac-magenta—a color not duplicated in other lavender roses. Medium-tall bush is clothed in dark green foliage.
Intrigue Floribunda 1984 *Photo above*	Purple-red	AARS 1984. Globular black-purple buds open to full, attractively ruffled, plum-colored blossoms with a powerful citrusy fragrance. Overall appearance is that of a small hybrid tea. Upright bush of medium height.
Lady X Hybrid Tea 1966 *Photo above*	Lavender-Pink	This one might win the prize for being the tallest and huskiest of the lavenders, but the color is the least blue. Long, elegant, pale lavender-pink buds unfurl gracefully to full, well-formed, lightly scented flowers.
Paradise* Hybrid Tea 1978 *Photo above*	Lavender and red blend	AARS 1979. Here is a distinctive color combination: silvery lavender petals are edged in ruby-red, the red tones spreading over more of the petal surfaces as the flowers age. Buds and flowers are beautifully formed; plant grows to medium height.
Pillow Talk Floribunda 1980 *Photo page 23*	Reddish lavender	Clusters of short, ovoid buds open to medium-size, fairly full, ruby-lavender blossoms with creamy petal backs. Moderately fragrant. Rounded, bushy plant of medium height sports attractive dark green foliage.
Smoky Hybrid Tea 1968	Lavender blend	The color is nearly impossible to describe, since it varies according to the weather: purple, smoky plum, raspberry, even a deep, smoldering burnt orange. Pointed buds and full, lightly fragrant blooms come on a plant of medium height.
Sterling Silver Hybrid Tea 1957	Silvery lavender	The rose that pushed lavenders into popularity, 'Sterling Silver' is still notable for its clear, silvery lavender color and intense old-rose scent. Attractive pointed buds and cup-shaped blooms come on a medium-size, moderately vigorous bush.

*Also available as a climber.

Altissimo

Blaze

America

Climbing Roses

NAME & TYPE*	COLOR	DESCRIPTION
Alchymist SC 1956	Yellow and pink blend	Blooms profusely during a long spring season, bearing extra-full, peonylike blossoms. Color is light yellow shading to orange in the flower center; petals are often tinted with pink. Very vigorous, with glossy bronze-tinted foliage.
Aloha CHT 1949	Two-tone pink	Plentiful dark, glossy foliage and restrained growth habit mark this as a good choice for a pillar rose or even a big free-standing shrub. The large, full-petaled flowers are rose-pink with darker petal backs.
Altissimo LCL 1966 *Photo above*	Bright red	Buds in small clusters open to spectacular velvety red, seven-petaled single flowers centered with clusters of yellow stamens. The glossy-leafed plant can serve both as a climber and, with pruning, as a tall shrub.
America LCL 1976 *Photo above*	Coral-pink	AARS 1976. Beautiful buds and large, full, highly fragrant, coral-pink blooms of the best hybrid tea form adorn these vigorous plants throughout the season. Can be grown upright, as a pillar rose.
American Pillar R 1908 *Photo page 22*	Carmine-pink	Lavish spring display features large clusters of half-dollar size carmine-pink blossoms, each with a white central eye. Glossy-leafed, ultra-vigorous plant has pliable, easily trained canes, is especially cold tolerant.
Belle Portugaise HG 1903	Light pink	In mild-winter regions, this rampant climber will cover a vast territory. Very early in spring, it produces moderately full long-stemmed, hybrid tea–type blooms from unusually long, tapered buds. Color is a soft, silvery pink.
Blaze LCL 1932 *Photo above*	Bright scarlet	Clusters of bright scarlet, 2- to 3-inch double flowers cover the plant over a long spring season, then continue in smaller bursts through summer and autumn. Slight fragrance. A trouble-free, indestructible plant.
Blossomtime LCL 1951	Two-tone pink	On the borderline between shrub and climber, this glossy-leafed rose can be used upright or trained horizontally. Blossoms of hybrid tea form, borne in small clusters, are very full, medium-size, in light pink with darker petal backs.

*Key to abbreviations: Climbing Hybrid Tea (CHT), Shrub-Climber (SC), Large-flowered Climber (LCL), Rambler (R), Hybrid Gigantea (HG), Kordesii Climber (KC), Climbing Tea (CT), Hybrid Bracteata (HB)

Climbing Mrs. Sam McGredy   Dortmund   Paul's Scarlet Climber

...Climbing Roses

NAME & TYPE*	COLOR	DESCRIPTION
Butterscotch (Jactan) LCL 1986	Tan-orange blend	The tan-orange flower color sets this rose apart from all others. Buds and moderately full flowers of hybrid tea style are borne in small clusters on a moderate climber clothed in semiglossy leaves.
Cl. Mrs. Sam McGredy CHT 1937 *Photos above, page 25*	Salmon blend	Flawless, classically tapered, copper-scarlet buds have salmon to apricot color on the insides of the petals. New growth is a show in itself: glossy plum-bronze, turning to dark green. Vigorous and very free flowering.
Cl. Snowbird CHT 1949	Creamy white	This climber captures much of the grace of old tea roses. Plentiful soft green foliage is a backdrop for lovely, pointed creamy white buds and sweetly fragrant, very full flowers that open fairly flat. Plant is very vigorous.
Don Juan LCL 1958	Deep crimson	A pillar-climber with 8- to 10-foot canes that grow upright. Velvety red buds of best hybrid tea form and size come singly or in small clusters on long stems. Flowers open well in all climates.
Dortmund KC 1955 *Photo above*	Cherry-red	A climber that also can be used as a ground cover or free-standing shrub. Outstanding, disease-proof foliage is a glossy, hollylike dark green; clustered single, cherry-red blooms have white centers.
Gloire de Dijon CT 1853	Buff and pink blend	A climbing tea rose (see page 10) differing in flower style from modern roses but resembling a climbing hybrid tea in growth and productivity. Plump buds open to very full, rather flat blooms combining buff, yellow, and pink tones.
Golden Showers LCL 1956	Daffodil-yellow	AARS 1957. Introduced as a pillar rose, but can be grown as a moderately large climber in mild regions. Pointed butter-yellow buds open to semidouble blooms of lighter yellow on a free-flowering plant with excellent glossy foliage.
Handel LCL 1965	Cream and pink	Use it as a climber or a pillar rose—either way, you'll get quantities of wavy-petaled, semidouble blossoms that open from clusters of attractive buds. Color is creamy pink, with each petal bordered in bright rose-pink.
High Noon CHT 1946	Golden yellow	AARS 1948. Similar in many respects to 'Golden Showers', this is a pillar rose or rampant climber, depending upon climate. Dark yellow buds are flushed with red, and the entire effect is more golden than pure yellow. Foliage is highly glossy.
Joseph's Coat LCL 1964 *Photos page 17, 51*	Red, orange, and yellow blend	This one is versatile: use it as a climber or as a free-standing shrub. The color changes as the blooms mature—from yellow in the plump buds, through orange and red shadings, and finally to crimson. Flowers come in floribundalike clusters. Glossy foliage.
Mermaid HB 1918	Soft yellow	A unique rose. Bright, light green leaves with a lacquerlike gloss cover the plant throughout the year, providing a backdrop for 4-inch, soft yellow single flowers. Very vigorous; use as large climber or free-standing shrub. Cold-tender.

*Key to abbreviations: Climbing Hybrid Tea (CHT), Shrub-Climber (SC), Large-flowered Climber (LCL), Rambler (R), Hybrid Gigantea (HG), Kordesii Climber (KC), Climbing Tea (CT), Hybrid Bracteata (HB)

Royal Gold

Royal Sunset

Joseph's Coat

NAME & TYPE*	COLOR	DESCRIPTION
New Dawn LCL 1930	Light pink	The first plant to be patented, and the first really cold-tolerant climbing rose having hybrid tea–type blooms. Small clusters of moderately full flowers are a slightly two-tone light pink. Can also be used as a shrub.
Paul's Scarlet Climber LCL 1916 *Photo page 50*	Bright red	An old favorite. Brilliant, unfading, double crimson-scarlet flowers (similar to those of 'Blaze') are borne in clusters. The vigorous, medium-size plant blooms in spring only, but profusely over a long period.
Piñata LCL 1978	Yellow and orange	Glossy foliage sets off floribunda-style golden yellow flowers edged and washed with orange-red. Growth is restrained, somewhat shrubby; use the plant as a small climber, pillar, or free-standing shrub.
Red Fountain LCL 1975	Deep red	A floribunda-style pillar rose or short climber that's derived from two other favorite climbers: 'Don Juan' and 'Blaze'. Clustered, medium-size, informal flowers are a velvety dark red, opening from buds that verge on black.
Rhonda LCL 1968	Coral-pink	Another restrained grower that can be used as a pillar rose or fanned out horizontally as a small climber. Globular buds in small clusters open to full, medium-size blossoms of warm deep pink. Foliage is glossy and dark green.
Royal Gold LCL 1957 *Photo above*	Golden yellow	Glowing yellow buds of perfect hybrid tea form are borne on this pillar rose or shrubby climber; plant is larger where winters are mild. Well-formed blooms come singly or in small clusters, retain color and good form when open.
Royal Sunset LCL 1960 *Photo above*	Orange blend	Basically orange buds of the best hybrid tea form and size open to large, fairly full, buff-apricot blooms that pale to a creamy peach in hot weather. Plant grows large in mild regions. Dark bronze-green, glossy leaves.
Sombreuil CT 1850	Creamy white	Short, plump buds open to creamy white (sometimes pink-flushed), flat, circular flowers intricately packed with countless petals. Glossy, dark green leaves on a modest-size, thorny plant that can be trained either as pillar or climber.
Spectra LCL 1983	Gold and red blend	Flowers of excellent hybrid tea style offer a continually changing color display. The shapely buds are tawny gold with a hint of red; maturing flowers are increasingly infused with red and pink. Dark, glossy foliage.
Tempo LCL 1975	Bright red	A free-blooming pillar type or short climber bearing floribundalike clusters of bright red, medium-size blossoms. Individual flowers are very full, opening from shapely dark red buds.
White Dawn LCL 1949	Pure white	The ruffled, medium-size, pure white blooms have the form of gardenias. A lavish spring display is followed by moderate bloom during summer, then another big burst in autumn. Especially vigorous plant with glossy leaves.

*Key to abbreviations: Climbing Hybrid Tea (CHT), Shrub-Climber (SC), Large-flowered Climber (LCL), Rambler (R), Hybrid Gigantea (HG), Kordesii Climber (KC), Climbing Tea (CT), Hybrid Bracteata (HB)

Beauty Secret

Kathy

Debut

Magic Carrousel

Black Jade

Miniature Roses

The following selection includes many of the miniatures rated highest in annual surveys conducted by the American Rose Society (see page 10). Height designations are based on the relative stature each plant will achieve when planted in the ground. Short (S) types reach 1½ feet; medium (M) kinds grow to 1½ to 2½ feet; and tall (T) types exceed 2½ feet. (If plants are grown in containers, these size differences will be less pronounced.)

Red & Red Bicolor

Beauty Secret, T. Lovely long, pointed buds open to semi-double blossoms. Dark green foliage. *Photo above.*

Black Jade, M. Dusky black-red buds of best hybrid tea form open to fairly large, full blossoms of velvety dark red. *Photo above.*

Debut, M. AARS 1989. Each ivory petal has a broad red edge. Pointed buds open to well-formed, moderately full blooms. *Photo above.*

Dreamglo, T. Hybrid tea–type buds and very full flowers have white petals edged and washed with red.

Fire Princess, M. Clusters of bright, fiery red-orange blooms. Both flowers and leaves are larger than average.

Kathy, M. Full, well-formed blossoms open from hybrid tea–type buds. Color is a rich red, dark yet bright. *Photo above.*

Libby, M. Well-formed buds open to semidouble white flowers heavily edged and shaded red.

Magic Carrousel, T. Striking color combination: white petals are precisely edged in red. Shapely buds. *Photo above.*

My Valentine, S. Clusters of short, pointed buds open to fairly small, rosette-shaped blossoms of rich red.

Over the Rainbow, M. Full, brilliant red blossoms are made all the brighter by yellow petal backs. Spreading plant.

Poker Chip, T. In both flowers and foliage, this looks like a scaled-down hybrid tea. Velvety scarlet petals are backed with yellow.

Scarlet Gem, M. Small, globular buds open to unfading bright scarlet flowers packed with petals. Glossy foliage.

Stars 'n' Stripes, M. Small hybrid tea–type flowers are striped red and white—no two alike. Light green leaves.

Toy Clown, M. Shapely white buds are tipped with red; open blooms are white with cerise petal edges. Large leaves.

Judy Fischer

Cupcake

Baby Darling

Peaches 'n' Cream

Pink

Antique Rose, T. Full, rather large, bright pink blossoms are reminiscent of some old garden roses. Dark, glossy leaves.

Baby Betsy McCall, M. Semidouble, half-dollar-size flowers open from hybrid tea–type buds. Compact plant.

Baby Cécile Brunner, T. A miniature version of 'Cécile Brunner', with perfect soft pink buds and full flowers.

Bo Peep, S. Small light pink flowers open from hybrid tea–type buds. Small leaves cover a compact plant.

Buttons 'n' Bows, M. Well-formed buds and flowers feature a two-tone combination of deep and lighter pink.

Choo-Choo Centennial, M. Sprays of small, very full, bicolor blooms in pink and white with darker pink shadings.

Cuddles, M. Shapely dark coral-pink buds and full open flowers are borne on an upright plant with dark foliage.

Cupcake, M. Clear cotton-candy-pink buds and blooms of best hybrid tea style, complemented by glossy leaves. *Photo above.*

Heidi, T. A moss rose in miniature. Typically "mossy" buds open to full, very fragrant, bright medium pink blossoms.

Janna, T. Backs of petals are white, edged in pink; insides are edged and infused with more pink.

Jean Kenneally, T. Good-sized flowers of perfect hybrid tea form, one to a stem, in soft apricot-pink.

Judy Fischer, M. Beautifully formed rose-pink buds open to half-dollar-size blossoms, each a perfect hybrid tea replica. *Photo above.*

Kathy Robinson, T. Pink on the inside, white on the outside. Beautifully formed buds and flowers.

Millie Walters, M. Full, rich reddish-coral blossoms are perfect miniatures of the best hybrid tea blooms.

Minnie Pearl, M. Long, shapely buds and open flowers of hybrid tea form are soft, warm pink with darker petal backs.

Peaches 'n' Cream, M. Beautiful buds and large flowers of finest hybrid tea quality in a blend of warm pink and cream. *Photo above.*

Rosmarin, M. Rounded buds unfold to rosette-shaped, light pink flowers with dark centers. Spreading plant. *Photo page 13.*

Trinket, S. Small in every way—flowers, foliage, plant size. Pointed buds; full, light pink blooms with pointed petals.

Valerie Jeanne, M. Clusters of very full blooms in an unusual deep magenta-pink open flat from ovoid buds. Glossy leaves.

Willie Winkie, S. Another small, fine-textured miniature. Globular buds produce very full, rose-pink blossoms.

...Miniature Roses

Orange & Multicolor

Baby Darling, M. Hybrid tea–style buds of apricot-orange expand to shapely, moderately full, 2-inch blossoms. *Photo page 53.*

Carnival Glass, T. Glossy, bronzy leaves complement the orange and yellow shades of the very full flowers.

Chattem Centennial, M. Heavy-blooming plant produces ovoid buds and full, flat flowers of brilliant orange-scarlet.

Chipper, M. Pink and orange tones in hybrid tea–style buds that open to full, half-dollar-size blossoms.

Holy Toledo, M. Petals of the full hybrid tea–type flowers are apricot-orange on the insides, yellow-orange on the backs.

Hula Girl, T. Pure bright orange, from the attractive buds to the open blooms of half-dollar size. *Photo page 55.*

Little Jackie, M. Light orange petals with yellow backs. Shapely buds and fragrant, moderately full blossoms.

Mary Marshall, T. Fairly large flowers open from flawless buds. Color is orange, with tints of red and yellow.

Orange Honey, M. Perfectly shaped gold-orange buds take on red tones as the moderately full flowers open and age. *Photo page 55.*

Orange Sunblaze, T. Full, rosette-shaped, clustered blossoms in a stunning bright orange verging on red.

Party Girl, S. Soft blend of salmon, apricot, yellow, and cream in well-formed, moderately full blooms. Upright plant.

Puppy Love, M. Both the hybrid tea–quality buds and moderately full flowers are a rich blend of orange, pink, and yellow.

Rainbow's End, M. Full, pointed yellow buds have red petal edges; as flowers age, petals are wholly suffused with red.

Rose Window, S. Glowing combination of yellow, orange, and pink in hybrid tea–type buds and moderately full blossoms.

Sheri Anne, M. Lovely buds in a brilliant hue that's more orange than 'Starina'. Semidouble blooms; spreading plant.

Starina, M. Faultless buds and open flowers of best hybrid tea style in vivid orange-scarlet. Glossy foliage. *Photo page 55.*

Yellow

Bojangles, M. Moderately full, 1½-inch blossoms are a clear, unshaded lemon-yellow. Glossy light green foliage. *Photo page 23.*

Rise 'n' Shine, M. Beautifully shaped golden buds open into large flowers, many on individual stems. Large leaves.

Yellow Doll, S. Shapely buds of pure, glowing yellow open to fairly large, full flowers. Short and spreading. *Photo page 55.*

White

Cinderella, M. Tiny buds and full, 1-inch blooms are pale pink in cool weather. Small leaves; compact, bushy plant.

Little Eskimo, T. Attractively pointed buds open to very full blooms with pointed petal tips. Semiglossy foliage.

Pacesetter, M. Long, pointed buds and shapely open flowers are perfect replicas of hybrid teas. Long stems, dark foliage.

Popcorn, M. Clustered globular buds pop open to tiny semi-double flowers with butter-yellow stamens. Rounded plant. *Photo page 55.*

Simplex, S. Open flowers are the major attraction: each is a starlike, five-petaled single bloom to 1½ inches across. *Photo page 55.*

Snow Bride, T. Perfect hybrid tea–type buds, one to each long stem, open to moderately full, lightly fragrant flowers.

Starglo, T. Full blooms of glowing creamy white feature pointed petal tips (the "star" in this rose's name).

Lavender

Angel Darling, S. Ruffled petals form a semidouble, white-centered lavender flower. Bushy plant has dark, glossy leaves.

Lavender Jade, T. Hybrid tea–type buds open to fragrant bicolor blooms—petals are lavender-mauve on the faces, ivory-white on the backs.

Lavender Jewel, T. Plump hybrid tea–style buds and full, fragrant blooms are soft lavender, sometimes touched magenta.

Lavender Lace, M. Its color is close to that of 'Sterling Silver'. Blooms are usually borne in clusters. Spreading plant.

Sweet Chariot, M. Clusters or small sprays of small, full, scented flowers in a blend of lavender and purple.

Winsome, T. Large, dark-foliaged plant bears perfect hybrid tea replicas in blended tones of dark purple and lavender.

Climbers

Candy Cane. White-striped pink flowers suggested the name. Clustered semidouble blooms come on a large-leafed plant.

Hi Ho. Full, half-dollar-size, deep pink flowers open from hybrid tea–type buds. Vigorous plant has large, glossy leaves.

Jeanne Lajoie. Clusters of small, full flowers in vivid medium pink on a vigorous climber with dark, glossy foliage.

Pink Cameo. Clusters of small, bright pink, hybrid tea–type buds open to moderately full flowers with wavy petal edges.

Red Cascade. Plant can grow as a ground cover or spill from a hanging basket. Blooms are small, full, dark red.

Red Wand. Globular buds open to full, light crimson blossoms that are sometimes borne in small clusters. Vigorous plant. *Photo page 21.*

Orange Honey

Starina

Hula Girl

Yellow Doll

Simplex

Popcorn

Constance Spry

Bonica '82

Ballerina

Shrub Roses

As explained on page 12, shrub roses are a heterogeneous lot, fitting none of the established classes. Flower and plant size vary considerably throughout the group, but all members serve well as flowering shrubs. Unless otherwise indicated, the roses described here flower repeatedly all year long. Actual plant size depends on climate and culture, but the relative heights indicated offer a good guide to placement.

Ballerina (1937). Single, white-centered pink flowers, borne in large clusters, resemble dogwood or apple blossoms in their airy charm. Upright, dense, glossy-leafed hybrid musk of medium height. *Photo above.*

Belinda (1936). A hybrid musk bearing large, phloxlike clusters of small, semidouble, bright pink blooms on a mounding, medium-tall plant. Glossy, disease-resistant foliage. Performs well in partial shade. *Photo page 12.*

Bonica '82 (1981). AARS 1987. Also sold as 'Bonica' and 'Meidomonac'. Dense, mounding plants of medium height cover themselves with large clusters of smallish, very full blooms in clear, soft pink. *Photos above, page 4.*

Buff Beauty (1939). Small clusters of medium-size, very full and shapely flowers in golden apricot fading to cream. A hybrid musk with large, bronzy leaves and an arching habit; can be used as a small climber.

Canterbury (1969). Large, intensely fragrant blooms, slightly more than single, in a warm shade of pink. Rounded bush of medium height. An "English Rose" (see page 13).

Carefree Beauty (1977). In plant habit and flower style, this one is like an extra-large floribunda. Long buds in small clusters open into semidouble, rich pink blooms; orange hips last over winter.

Champlain (1982). Dark red double flowers in floribundalike clusters adorn a bushy, medium-size, rounded plant that endures Canadian winters with no special protection.

Constance Spry (1961). Rich pink flowers in old-rose style: large, full, and cupped. Distinctive scent; blooms in spring only. Grow as a climber or prune to a large shrub. An "English Rose" (see page 13). *Photo above.*

Cornelia (1925). Elongated, phloxlike clusters of small, rosette-shaped flowers in coral-pink fading to creamy pink. A glossy-leafed hybrid musk, this one can serve as an arching shrub or a small climber. Grows well in partial shade.

Country Dancer (1973). Looks like a moderately full-flowered, bright pink floribunda. Medium-size plant with disease-resistant foliage; developed in Iowa to withstand prairie winters with little or no protection.

Penelope

Thérèse Bugnet

Kathleen

Erfurt (1939). Creamy ivory petals broadly edged in dark rose-pink give the large, slightly more than single blossoms a luminous look. Arching canes form a medium-tall, mounding plant clothed in bronze-tinted foliage.

Golden Wings (1956). Tall, upright plant with light green foliage bears large single or nearly single flowers in bright light yellow with contrasting red-brown stamens.

John Franklin (1980). Looks like a large floribunda: medium-tall, bushy plant with large clusters of wavy-petaled semidouble flowers in bright medium red. Endures Canadian winters with no protection.

Kathleen (1922). Blush-pink, apple blossom–style single blooms, each about half-dollar size, are borne in clusters on a vigorous, arching bush. Like other hybrid musks, this one performs well in part shade. *Photo above.*

Lilian Austin (1973). Arching, glossy-leafed plant; clusters of fragrant, moderately full, wavy-petaled blossoms of salmon pink with gold tints. An "English Rose" (see page 13).

Nymphenburg (1954). Grow as a loose bush, pillar rose, or restrained climber. Clusters of highly fragrant, moderately full blooms combine salmon-pink and orange with tinges of pink and yellow. Foliage is dark and glossy.

Penelope (1924). Salmon-orange buds open to fluffy, semidouble, 3-inch, creamy buff blossoms in moderate-size clusters. Coral-pink hips appear in autumn and winter. A hybrid musk, and a good hedge plant. *Photo above.*

Prairie Princess (1972). Long, pointed buds open to ruffled clear pink blossoms of moderate size and fullness. Tall bush endures prairie winters with little or no protection.

Sally Holmes (1976). Large, single, pink-blushed white flowers resembling apple blossoms are carried in clusters on a tall, somewhat rounded plant with dark, glossy foliage.

Scarlet Meidiland (1987). Clusters of small, brilliant red blossoms cover a rounded plant of medium height. Small, dark leaves. Performs well in partial shade.

Sea Foam (1964). Clustered full, rosette-shaped blossoms billow like creamy white foam against a sea of dark, glossy leaves. Mounding, spreading bush of medium height.

Simplicity (1979). Classed as a floribunda but promoted as a shrub, this tall, bushy plant is easily maintained as a hedge. Long, pointed buds produce semidouble, bright pink blossoms in small clusters. *Photo page 27.*

Thérèse Bugnet (1950). Slender near-red buds open to lilac-pink double flowers with a fluffy, informal quality. Withstands Canadian winters without protection. *Photo above.*

The Yeoman (1969). Especially fragrant, wavy-petaled flowers of warm pink with gold tints open cup shaped or flat. Compact, upright bush reaches medium height.

Will Scarlet (1948). Clusters of semidouble, bright bluish-scarlet blooms; autumn flowers form glossy orange-red hips that look decorative in winter. A tall, upright hybrid musk.

La Reine Victoria

Rose de Meaux

Celestial

Old Garden Roses

Aside from their value as antiques, many of the older roses are fine garden subjects. You'll find a discussion of general class distinctions on pages 6 to 11. As a guide to placement in the garden, we have noted relative plant heights. These heights equate over all classes; a tall alba, for example, will potentially reach the same height as a tall hybrid perpetual.

Alba

Celestial (before 1848). Moderately full, distinctly scented blossoms in a clear, soft, milky pink are displayed against gray-green leaves on a tall, upright plant. *Photo above.*

Félicité Parmentier (before 1834). Packed with petals, the pale pink blossoms open cupped, then reflex to a rounded shape as they fade to nearly white. Medium-size plant; gray-toned foliage. *Photo page 7.*

Great Maiden's Blush (before 1738). Also called *Rosa alba incarnata*. A large, arching shrub well clothed with gray-green leaves, this one bears full blossoms of a milky blush-pink. 'Small Maiden's Blush' is nearly identical but produces slightly smaller flowers on a plant about two-thirds the size of 'Great Maiden's Blush'.

Königin von Dänemark (1826). As each bud opens, countless deep pink petals expand to a cup-shaped blossom which reflexes as it matures, its color fading to pale pink at the margins. Medium-tall, arching bush has coarse foliage with a blue-gray cast.

Bourbon

Honorine de Brabant (date unknown). Light pink to nearly white petals are irregularly striped purplish pink to violet, but the effect is harmonious rather than garish. Full, cupped blossoms are borne on a tall, thickly foliaged plant with few thorns.

La Reine Victoria (1872). Also called 'Reine Victoria'. Shell-like, silky petals form cupped, globular, fragrant, medium-size flowers in rich pink. Small clusters of blossoms appear on a tall, slender bush that bears elegant-looking leaves of soft green. 'Mme. Pierre Oger' is a creamy pink sport. *Photo above.*

Louise Odier (1851). Full-petaled, cupped to camellialike blossoms are bright, deep pink with a pronounced fragrance. Tall, vigorous plant may also be used as a pillar, though the heavy bloom clusters may weigh down the stems.

Mme. Isaac Pereire (1881). Everything about this rose says "big"—including its fragrance. Full-petaled blooms of intense purplish pink are backed by large leaves on a plant so vigorous that it is better used as a small climber.

Souvenir de la Malmaison (1843). So full of petals are the flat, circular, soft pink flowers that they might pass for centifolias. In fact, the flowers are so double that they may not open fully in damp climates. The rounded bush is medium to medium-tall in height; the climbing sport is exceptionally vigorous. *Photo page 8.*

Hermosa

Rosa Mundi

Leda

Zéphirine Drouhin (1868). Thornless stems are just one of the selling points. Medium-size, shapely buds open to cerise-pink semidouble flowers with white centers; new growth is plum-purple. Use plant as moderate climber or large shrub.

Centifolia

Crested Moss (1827). Also called *Rosa centifolia cristata* and 'Chapeau de Napoleon'. Not a true moss rose, this has an elaborately fringed calyx. From this rococo cocoon emerges a full, fragrant, bright silvery pink blossom with a cupped shape. Light green foliage on a lax, medium-tall plant.

Fantin-Latour (date unknown). Sumptuous large, full blossoms of soft but rich pink open cup shaped, then reflex to show a buttonlike center. Handsome dark green foliage clothes a tall, vigorous, upright to arching plant. *Photo page 7.*

Paul Ricault (1845). Blooms profusely, bearing cupped, fragrant, rich pink to cerise blossoms densely packed with petals. Medium-tall plant.

Rose de Meaux (1789). One of several dwarf centifolias. The full, pomponlike, bright pink flowers are just 1½ inches across; the upright plant is correspondingly short. Light green foliage. *Photo page 58.*

Tour de Malakoff (1856). Fragrant, very full, peonylike blossoms start out light pink with shadings of crimson and violet, then quickly fade to grayish mauve. To show off its large, heavy flowers, this tall, lax-growing plant needs some support; it can be grown as a small climber.

China

Cramoisi Supérieur (1832). Also known as 'Agrippina'. "Glowing" describes this China: brilliant velvety crimson petals form moderately full, cupped blooms like smallish floribundas. Plant is angular, twiggy, to medium height. *Photo page 8.*

Hermosa (1840). Bushy shrub reaches medium height, grows taller in time. Gray-green foliage forms a backdrop for the numerous clear lilac-pink blossoms, each a moderately small, full flower with cupped, globular old-rose form. *Photo above.*

Mutabilis (date unknown). Also called 'Tipo Ideale'. A plant in full flower resembles a collection of variously colored butterflies: 3-inch single flowers open buff-yellow, change to warm pink, then darken to crimson in sunny weather. Twiggy bush is typically rounded, but may become tall and spreading. Mahogany-colored new growth.

Old Blush (from China, 1789). Originally called 'Parson's Pink China'. Informal semidouble blossoms of clear medium pink take on darker red tints in sunshine. Upright plants flower continuously, can become tall if pruned lightly or not at all. *Photo page 29.*

Damask

Celsiana (before 1750). Intense fragrance emanates from large semidouble blooms composed of silky, ruffled, soft pink petals. Small clusters of flowers adorn a somewhat lax, moderately tall bush with gray-green leaves.

Paul Neyron

Deuil de Paul Fontaine

...Old Garden Roses

Leda (date unknown). Crimson markings on the tips of the blush to white petals have given this one the common name Painted Damask. Extremely full and symmetrical flowers. Dark green foliage clothes a compact bush of medium height. *Photo page 59.*

Marie Louise (before 1813). Grown at Malmaison and still treasured for the magnificence of its very large, very full and fragrant blossoms. Each deep carmine-pink bloom is centered with a buttonlike eye of smaller petals. Medium-size, lax-growing bush is further weighted down by its heavy flowers.

Mme. Hardy (1832). Its special beauty is in the open flowers: cupped to flat, each packed with symmetrically arranged petals around a green center. Clusters of fragrant white blossoms come on a moderately tall plant with dark leaves.

Rosa damascena bifera. Often called Autumn Damask or Rose of Castile. Unlike many other old roses, this flowers more than once annually. Slender buds with notably long sepals open to highly scented, clear pink, loose blossoms. The plant is large, open, and thorny, with light yellowish gray-green foliage. *Photo page 7.*

Gallica

Cardinal de Richelieu (1840). Nearly thornless stems clothed in smooth green leaves make up a rounded, dense bush bearing small clusters of nearly ball-shaped flowers. Rounded buds open to rosy violet blooms with shell-like petals; as blossoms expand, petals turn rich purple with silvery reverses.

Charles de Mills (date unknown). Heady fragrance rises from full-petaled, flat crimson flowers with tints of purple, lavender, and pink among the folded petals. The compact, medium-tall bush has few thorns.

Rosa gallica officinalis. Often called Apothecary Rose. Cheery semidouble, cherry-crimson blossoms with contrasting yellow stamens cover a dense, leafy plant of medium height. An historic rose, presumed to be the "Red Rose of Lancaster" in the Wars of the Roses.

Rosa Mundi (before 1581). Also known as *Rosa gallica versicolor.* A sport of *R.g. officinalis* (above) with striped flowers: crimson and palest pink assort in various stripes, dashes, and stipples. *Photo page 59.*

Tuscany Superb (before 1837). Wavy petals that look cut from maroon velvet form a semidouble blossom around a central cluster of golden stamens. Rich green leaves cover an upright, medium-size bush with few thorns. *Photo page 7.*

Hybrid Perpetual

Baronne Prévost (1842). Like a Portland rose, but larger. Full, cupped to flat or slightly recurved, bright rose-pink blossoms usually have a central buttonlike eye. Upright bush carries somewhat coarse leaves on thorny stems. *Photo page 21.*

Frau Karl Druschki (1901). Long, pointed buds, sometimes tinged pink, always unfurl to full, sparkling white blossoms that open well even in damp regions. Extremely vigorous.

Maréchal Niel

Comte de Chambord

Catherine Mermet

Général Jacqueminot (1853). The historic Jack Rose, an ancestor of virtually all contemporary red hybrid teas, features full, slightly cupped, highly fragrant blossoms of cherry-crimson that open from shapely darker red buds. Vigorous, tall plant.

Mrs. John Laing (1887). Plump but shapely buds with curled-back petal edges open to full, rather cupped, fragrant flowers on strong stems. Tall, vigorous (but not rangy) bush with small thorns and light green foliage. *Photo page 9.*

Paul Neyron (1869). Though the nickname "cabbage rose" is usually applied to centifolias, the term is just as appropriate for this variety. Huge blooms of deep, slightly bluish pink, loaded with row upon row of petals, unfold from fat buds. Plant is tall, somewhat arching, and nearly thornless, with lettuce-green foliage. *Photo page 60.*

Reine des Violettes (1860). Aside from its repeat-flowering ability, this has little in common with other hybrid perpetuals and instead resembles a gallica. Full, flat flowers with a central buttonlike eye start out carmine-red, then quickly fade to shades of magenta, violet, and lavender. Medium-tall plant has gray-green leaves on nearly thornless stems.

Moss

Alfred de Dalmas (1855). Also called 'Mousseline'. Creamy pink flowers—moderately full, with shell-shaped petals—have a porcelainlike delicacy and a pleasant perfume. Low, spreading plant flowers continuously.

Communis (about 1696). Also known as Common Moss and *Rosa centifolia muscosa*. This is the original moss rose—a highly scented, full-petaled, pink centifolia that opens cupped to flat. Spring bloom comes on a moderately tall, open plant.

Crested Moss. See Centifolia (page 59).

Deuil de Paul Fontaine (1873). Round, mossy buds open to 2-inch flowers packed with petals of an unusual purplish red with brown shading. Thorny, medium-size plant flowers repeatedly. *Photo page 60.*

Gloire des Mousseux (1852). Buds heavily cloaked in green "moss" unfold to really large, deep pink flowers that pale to lighter tones at the edges. Spring-flowering plant is of medium height, upright, with light green foliage.

Salet (1854). The steadiest bloomer of the repeat-flowering moss roses, featuring a moderate amount of "moss" and an informal, full, deep pink blossom. Bush is of medium height, with soft green leaves and few thorns. *Photo page 5.*

Noisette

Alister Stella Gray (1894). Shapely yellow buds in clusters open to full, medium-size, orange-centered flowers that fade to cream. Very vigorous, shrubby climber.

Blush Noisette (1817). The original Noisette rose. Clusters of small, rounded buds and full, pale pink blossoms are borne on a mounding semi-climbing plant. *Photo page 9.*

All-America Rose Selections

Sweet Surrender

In 1938, leading rose growers founded the nonprofit organization AARS—All-America Rose Selections, Inc.—both to establish a test program for new rose varieties and to publicize those which proved especially worthy. Today, the AARS testing system operates nationwide, evaluating roses in 24 accredited test gardens located in 19 states. The AARS Test Garden Committee oversees each of these sites to guarantee high standards of rose culture that are comparable from one garden to the next.

To qualify for an AARS award, a rose must first be entered in the trials. Multiple plants go to each designated test garden, where they are grown for 2 years and evaluated for beauty, distinctiveness, disease resistance, vigor, growth habit, and productivity. When the 2-year test period ends, the AARS winners are determined by a secret-ballot election tabulating the results from all the gardens. Plants of the winning rose or roses are then shipped to approved AARS display gardens (there are currently over 130) throughout the country; here, the public may admire the prize-winners in the year their awards are announced.

Thanks to the rigorous test system, AARS roses are consistently top-quality plants that turn in good performances virtually everywhere. For this reason, such roses offer novices a particularly satisfactory introduction to the joys of rose growing. Nonetheless, the absence of an AARS designation does not automatically indicate an inferior rose. First, because not all new varieties are entered in the AARS trials, AARS-worthy roses can reach the market without AARS testing. And second, some roses are excellent performers in some climates or regions, but are outclassed by other varieties in other areas.

For more detailed information and a list of AARS display gardens, contact AARS, 221 N. La Salle, Chicago, IL 60601.

… Old Garden Roses

Lamarque (1830). Elegant, medium green, pointed leaves clothe a vigorous, far-reaching climber that is generous with its sweet-scented blossoms. Medium-size, clustered blossoms of creamy white to palest lemon open from shapely buds.

Maréchal Niel (1864). A tea-Noisette, beloved since its introduction for its large, beautifully shaped, highly fragrant blossoms of soft medium yellow on pendant stems. Plant needs a warm climate, good care for best performance. *Photo page 61.*

Mme. Alfred Carrière (1879). A big, vigorous plant with plentiful gray-green foliage, this one can be used as a climber or kept as a large, arching shrub. Moderately large, full, sweet-scented flowers are blush-white to light salmon-pink.

Rêve d'Or (1869). Plenty of semiglossy green foliage covers a vigorous, freely branching, climbing plant. Fairly large, moderately full, shapely blossoms are bountifully produced throughout the year; color varies from buff-apricot to gold.

Portland

Comte de Chambord (1860). Old-rose-style flowers feature large outer petals that cradle a multitude of folded and rolled smaller petals; blooms are cool pink, highly fragrant. Upright plant to medium height. Elongated leaflets. *Photo page 61.*

Marquise Boccella (1842). Also called 'Jacques Cartier'. Reminiscent of 'Comte de Chambord' (above), but the medium-size flowers are expanded and reflexed (rather than cupped to flat), with a central button of petals. Upright plant; light foliage.

Rose du Roi (1815). The founding father of the hybrid perpetual class, this is a bush of modest size bearing full, fragrant, loose blossoms in crimson with lighter and darker shadings. Bushy plant with elongated leaflets. *Photo page 8.*

Tea

Catherine Mermet (1869). Pearly light pink buds and moderately full open flowers are of the best hybrid tea shape. Upright, tall plant. *Photo page 61.*

Duchesse de Brabant (1857). Tall, rounded, dense plant constantly produces cupped, moderately full flowers with shell-shaped petals. The usual color is medium pink; 'Mme. Joseph Schwartz' is a sport with pink-blushed ivory flowers.

Lady Hillingdon (1910). Decorative plum-purple new growth and stems harmonize well with large, moderately full, saffron-yellow blossoms that open from long, pointed buds. Upright, spreading bush is tall and rather open.

Maman Cochet (1893). Large hybrid tea–type buds of warm pink develop into very full, light pink blossoms with cream shadings. Tall, spreading plant. 'White Maman Cochet' is creamy ivory with pink on outer petals.

Mons. Tillier (1891). Opening from plump red buds, the flat, circular blossoms are packed with petals in old-rose style, but in shades of warm dark pink with gold, brick-red, and lilac tints. Lustrous, disease-proof foliage on a tall, rounded, especially dense plant. *Photo page 9.*

Harison's Yellow *Pink Grootendorst* *Rosa foetida bicolor*

Species & Species Hybrids

The selection of roses presented here includes both garden-worthy species and an assortment of hybrids that are, for the most part, first-generation offspring of species. For each hybrid, we have noted the parent species; for species roses, we've listed any widely used common names. Height designations are relative, since absolute size depends on climate and culture.

Blanc Double de Coubert (1892). Hybrid rugosa. Loose, fairly full, pure white flowers have poppylike petal texture; orange hips develop after flowers fade. Medium-tall, spreading plant features plentiful dark, rugosa-type foliage.

Frau Dagmar Hartopp (1914). Hybrid rugosa. Also known as 'Fru Dagmar Hastrup'. Fragrant, clear pink single blossoms and red hips appear throughout the growing season on a compact, medium-tall plant with plentiful rugosa-type foliage.

Frühlingsmorgen (1942). Hybrid spinosissima. Tall, arching bush with dark foliage. Blooms in spring, bearing large, yellow single flowers edged in cherry-pink and centered with maroon stamens. Autumn display of bright red hips.

Harison's Yellow (1830). Foetida-spinosissima hybrid. In spring, bushes are covered in clouds of small, sulfur-yellow double blossoms on a tall, strong plant with dark, thorny canes and fernlike foliage. An historic rose, brought from the East by pioneers and now found in old towns throughout the West. *Photo above.*

Nevada (1927). Hybrid moyesii. Early in spring, the long, arching canes carry 4-inch, nearly single, pink-tinted white blossoms all along their length; in later months, bloom is less profuse. Light green leaves and dark stems on a tall, spreading bush. 'Marguerite Hilling' is pink sport.

Pink Grootendorst (1923). Hybrid rugosa. Fringed petal edges give the small pink blossoms the appearance of carnations. Plentiful clusters of flowers from spring through autumn on a medium-tall bush with foliage similar to that of *Rosa rugosa*. *Photo above.*

Rosa banksiae. Lady Banks Rose. In mild-winter regions, this is one of spring's harbingers. Rampantly climbing, green-stemmed plants with narrow green leaves cover themselves with clustered quarter-size blossoms early in the season. The scentless double yellow form is more widely planted than the fragrant double white type.

Rosa foetida bicolor. Austrian Copper. The spring landscape offers no brighter show: single blossoms are brilliant orange on petal faces, golden yellow on the backs. Small bright green leaves appear on prickly, upright, moderately tall canes. *Photo above.*

Rosa roxburghii. Chestnut Rose. Bristly, burrlike calyx from which the bud emerges gave this species its common name. Large, full, flat flowers of vivid, cool pink bloom in spring on a medium-tall bush bearing locustlike leaves.

Rosa rugosa. The disease-proof, semiglossy foliage is distinctly textured or ribbed (rugose), a feature possessed by many of the species' hybrids. Medium-tall, bushy plants flower throughout the growing season, setting large orange or red hips during that period. 'Alba' has single white flowers; those of 'Rubra' are purplish red.

Stanwell Perpetual (1838). Hybrid spinosissima. Full, damask-type blossoms of blush pink appear from spring through autumn on a twiggy plant with small grayish-green leaves. Canes arch over to make a rounded, medium-tall bush.

Consistent, timely care—including periodic fertilizing—results in a flourishing rose garden. Here, floribunda 'Sarabande' receives fertilizer as one bloom cycle is on the wane.

The Art of Growing Roses

To grow roses successfully, you need to understand a few basic rules, then apply them with a measure of intuition—the "green thumb" that identifies all good gardeners. These final pages present a primer of good rose care, giving you the fundamental rules you'll adjust to suit the particular characteristics of your site, soil, and climate.

A first step in raising beautiful roses is, of course, choosing the right location for the rose garden. For ideas and inspiration, see pages 16 to 27. Once you've decided where to grow your roses and studied a few tips for selecting top-grade plants (pages 66 to 68), you'll turn your attention to how to grow them.

Soil will be your first concern: what type of soil is present in your garden, and how should it be modified to best suit your roses? From preparing the soil, you'll progress to planting, then to watering, learning about efficient, convenient watering systems as well as your roses' basic water needs. Through the year, you'll be spending some time on fertilizing and pest and disease control, and certainly on pruning. If you live in a cold-winter climate, you'll need information on methods for protecting roses during freezing weather. And when you've become truly hooked on rose growing (as you're bound to), you'll want to explore techniques for starting new plants on your own.

Shopping Wisely for Roses

You'll need to consider more than flower color when you shop for roses—the plants you choose must perform well in your climate and suit your garden in overall size and growth habit. You'll also need to decide *where* to shop: should you buy from mail-order sources or from local nurseries, supermarkets, or garden centers?

Which varieties to choose

On pages 30 to 63, you'll find vital statistics for 359 rose varieties, plus color photographs of 102 favorites. From these listings, you can make some preliminary choices for your garden—but before you buy, you'll need to narrow down your picks to those that will flourish in your region. Local rose growers can provide you with plenty of information on this score, and conversations with neighbors will probably yield at least a limited list of sure performers. A visit to a nearby public garden (see pages 94 and 95) is helpful, too: you can examine both newer rose varieties and satisfactory old favorites, and see first hand which sorts do best in your climate.

Bare-root or container-grown roses

Roses for garden planting are sold throughout the year. During the dormant season (late autumn through early spring), you'll find bare-root bushes; in the warmer months, you can buy growing plants in containers. In either form—bare-root or pot-grown—the roses you buy may be *budded* or *own-root* plants. In budded kinds (the majority of roses sold), growth eyes of the desired variety are budded (see page 92) onto a second rose, called the *understock*. All understocks are carefully chosen varieties with good root systems that will thrive in a wide range of soils and climates.

Own-root plants, as the name implies, grow on their own roots rather than an understock. Most own-root plants (virtually all miniatures, for example) are raised from cuttings. Others are "micropropagated"—that is, grown from individual cells, initially under laboratory conditions.

Ultimately, it makes no difference whether the roses you buy are budded or own-root: either can yield fine results. Budded plants do offer somewhat more uniform root quality than own-root types, but an own-root plant killed to ground level will regrow as the same rose, not as the understock. And though budded plants are usually larger than own-root types to start out with, the latter can become just as husky in a year or two.

Bare-root roses. Dormant bare-root specimens account for most of the roses marketed each year. In the dormant

---

Bare-root Quality Standards

The bare-root plants you buy are rated according to standards established by the American Association of Nurserymen, with each grade designated by a number: 1, 1½, or 2. The specifications for each of these grades may differ slightly depending upon the type of rose—hybrid tea, grandiflora, floribunda, polyantha, climber, old garden rose, species, shrub type—but in all cases, the canes measured to determine the grade should originate within 3 inches of the bud union.

When you select bare-root roses, keep in mind that the measurements expressed in the grading standards describe the plant *as it is dug from the field*. The grower, packager, or nurseryman will very often reduce the cane length for more convenient shipping or handling, but the cane diameter will give you some indication whether the plant originally qualified for the grade noted. Some of the smaller-growing roses may seem barely to meet the No. 1 standards, but this size is natural for them—they'll never have canes equal to those of husky giants like 'Queen Elizabeth'.

No. 1 grade. Hybrid teas and grandifloras must have three or more strong canes, at least two of which are 1½ feet long or longer. No. 1 floribundas should meet the same specifications, but their canes need be only 15 inches long. No. 1 polyanthas must have four or more canes at least a foot long; climbers need three or more canes of at least 2 feet.

No. 1½ grade. Hybrid teas and grandifloras need two or more strong canes of at least 15 inches long. Floribundas should have two canes that measure 14 inches or more. Climbers must have two 1½-foot canes. Polyanthas that don't meet No. 1 standards aren't graded.

No. 2 grade. Hybrid teas, grandifloras, and climbers—the only types you're ever likely to find in this grade—need have only two canes of 1 foot or longer. These plants are strictly a gamble: they may well be the runts of the 2-year-old field which produced the No. 1 plants also being offered.

---

state, the plants require less care than actively growing roses: they need only be kept moist and protected from extremes of temperature. To prevent dehydration during shipping, mail-order suppliers enclose the plants in polyethylene bags or encase the roots in a moistened lightweight material such as sawdust. Retail nurseries may hold quantities of bare-root bushes in beds of sawdust; supermarkets and some nurseries offer plants individually root-wrapped in a moistened fibrous material.

Bare-root roses present just one notable drawback: they're available for planting during the least appealing time of year for gardening. But for many gardeners, the advantages of bare-root planting far outweigh the discomfort of working outdoors in cold, wet weather. Bare-root roses cost less and offer a much greater range of choices than container-grown types; they're also easier to plant.

Container-grown roses.

Despite their relatively high price and (usually) limited selection compared to bare-root roses, container-grown plants offer numerous benefits: you can see that the plant is alive and healthy, examine its flower color and form, and tell something about its foliage color and disease resistance. If any roses in your garden have died over the winter, container-grown plants will fill in the gaps quickly; and, of course, they'll add instant color to a new rose garden. Perhaps the chief drawback to container-grown roses is that you can't see the roots—but if the canes and leaves look healthy and vigorous, it's almost always a safe bet that the plant is just as healthy *beneath* the soil surface.

When you buy flowering roses in containers, keep these points in mind:

■ Do your shopping during the first flush of bloom in spring, when you're assured of the widest possible selection and the chance to view each rose's blossoms. If possible, avoid buying in summer: not only do nursery plants look their worst then, but new plants have a hard time getting established in hot summer weather.

■ Unless you're buying miniatures or micropropagated plants, purchase only bushes planted earlier in the year from bare-root stock. Under nursery conditions, container-grown roses held over from previous years inevitably suffer from their prolonged confinement. Tell-tale signs of age include pruning scars from past years (often accompanied by dieback below the cuts) and dead canes or branches with twiggy growth attached.

■ Buy your roses in the largest containers offered, preferably in 3- to 5-gallon cans, paper pots, or other containers. Roses in gallon cans or small flower pots (miniatures excepted) may have been root-pruned to fit these more cramped quarters.

Where to buy roses

It's easy to buy roses—you'll see them in mail-order brochures, nurseries, garden centers, even supermarkets. And if you shop carefully, any of these outlets can provide you with good-quality plants.

Mail-order sources.

Mail-order rose specialists offer both convenience—you just wait for the plants to come to you—and a greater selection than any other source. Your choices will always include the very newest hybrids, and some growers make a point of keeping old favorites in stock as well. A number of specialists sell primarily or exclusively old garden roses, species, and shrub types rarely found in local nurseries. It's true that shopping by mail doesn't allow you to pick out each plant in person—but because their success depends entirely upon your satisfaction, reputable dealers will ship only first-class plants. (For more on mail-order sources, see page 68.)

Though planting times vary throughout the country from autumn through spring (see page 73), the earlier you order, the more certain you are to receive your first choices. It's best to make your selections soon after catalogues arrive, ideally before the December holidays. To give your new roses the longest possible growing period in your garden, ask that the plants be delivered early in your region's bare-root planting season; most large mail-order growers have cold-storage facilities, enabling them to send you dormant, well-ripened bushes at the optimal planting time for your region. If you do end up placing a late order, it's best to list a few acceptable substitutions yourself rather than leave the choice of possible alternates to the seller. This way, you avoid receiving as a substitute a rose you already have or one you don't care for.

Nurseries.

The particular roses stocked by your nearby nursery depend on who does the buying, but you'll typically find the most recent All-America winners (see page 62) as well as the standard, time-tested varieties. In addition, local nurseries are likely to sell any roses especially suited to your regional climate, regardless of their performance elsewhere. Bare-root nursery roses are usually heeled into beds of sawdust, so you can pick out plants with good, healthy canes; if you see that a plant's root system has been badly damaged, you can make another choice on the spot.

Supermarkets.

For convenience, the supermarket can't be beaten—you can stock your garden and your pantry shelves at the same time. Though there won't be a vast assortment from which to choose, you can usually count on finding old favorites of past decades as well as current top-rated patented roses.

The primary problem involved in buying supermarket roses is simply that you can't see the root system: inevitably, the roots are enclosed in long, narrow bags filled with a moistened fibrous material and tied just below the bud union. The canes are always on view, either swathed in a transparent plastic bag or dipped in wax to retain moisture. If the canes look healthy—not shriveled or discolored, with eyes plump and ready to grow but not growing—you can consider the plant a good risk. Sometimes, however, major roots may be broken in digging or packaging, and you won't learn about the problem until you unwrap the rose just before planting. Such plants may need an extra year or two to rebuild their root systems before they put on their best show in your garden.

◆ Shopping

You may also encounter a second difficulty with roses from the supermarket: a disappointingly high percentage of them may be incorrectly labeled, a fact you'll discover only when the plants leaf out and bloom. If you have your heart set on a specific variety, you're more likely to be satisfied if you buy from a mail-order firm or retail nursery.

One general tip for buying packaged rose plants: do it while they are still *new* on the supermarket shelves. Those with plastic-wrapped canes are well protected against the drying indoor atmosphere, but because the plastic acts as a miniature greenhouse, these plants often begin to grow soon after being set out on the shelves. Try to plant your roses right after purchase; if you can't, see "Holding methods for plants" (page 72).

Should you, despite all precautions, find yourself with sprouted plants to set out, just cut the shoots back to ¼-inch stubs. This will prevent the new shoots from using up moisture in the plants before the roots are established enough to replenish it.

Roses by Mail

Lavishly illustrated with color photographs and filled with enticing descriptions, mail-order rose catalogues have an undeniable allure. Even if your local nursery is well stocked with modern roses, you may be tempted by the wares of mail-order suppliers. Many firms carry a wide variety of hybrid teas, grandifloras, floribundas, and climbers, usually including the latest AARS winners and other recent introductions; you are also likely to find a number of reliable old favorites catalogued. Other suppliers make a special point of offering exotic new varieties from overseas that you won't find in the general nursery trade.

Fanciers of old garden roses, species, and shrub types will probably *have* to shop by mail, since very few retail outlets keep these roses in stock. It's true that you may be able to find some of the older sorts thriving in cemeteries and old or abandoned farmsteads, then grow them from cuttings (see page 92); but a far wider (and more identifiable) selection is offered in the brochures of the mail-order specialists listed below. Many of these suppliers have tapped European old rose sources and have brought some truly historic and attractive kinds back into cultivation.

Suppose, though, that you know the roses you want, old or modern, yet have no idea which supplier sells them? The annually published *Combined Rose List* can answer your questions: it provides an index of all roses available in the United States and Canada, as well as from British and other European suppliers. The roses are listed alphabetically; following each name is a code showing which growers propagate the rose. Also indicated are the rose's class, its originator and year of introduction, its trademark name, synonyms (if any), an abbreviated color classification, and a patent number (if the rose is patented). Copies of the *Combined Rose List* are available from Beverly R. Dobson, 215 Harriman Road, Irvington, NY 10533, at a cost of $10 each.

Mail-order sources for old roses. The following nurseries offer representative old roses of all classes.

The Antique Rose Emporium (catalogue $2)
Route 5, Box 143
Brenham, TX 77833

Heritage Rosarium (catalogue $1)
211 Haviland Mill Road
Brookeville, MD 20833

Heritage Rose Gardens (catalogue $1)
16831 Mitchell Creek Drive
Fort Bragg, CA 95437

High Country Rosarium
1717 Downing Street
Denver, CO 80218

Historical Roses
1657 West Jackson Street
Painesville, OH 44077

Hortico, Inc.
723 Robson Road, R.R. 1
Waterdown, Ontario L0R 2H0
Canada

Lowe's Own-Root Nursery (catalogue $2)
6 Sheffield Road
Nashua, NH 03062

Pickering Nurseries, Inc.
670 Kingston Road
Pickering, Ontario L1V 1A6
Canada

Roses of Yesterday & Today (catalogue $2)
802 Brown's Valley Road
Watsonville, CA 95076

Know Your Soil

All soils are composed of mineral particles formed by the natural breakdown of some sort of rock. These particles don't fit together seamlessly: there are pore spaces between them. The spaces are filled with air when the soil is dry; when it is dampened, water fills the spaces and coats each particle. As the water continues to move down through the soil, air re-enters the pore spaces, but the soil particles remain coated with a film of water. This air-water interchange is vital to the health of a rose's roots: they need soil that is constantly moist, yet fast draining enough that the pore spaces don't remain filled with water for any length of time. In waterlogged soil, roots will simply suffocate, since they can't get the oxygen they require to function.

Soil types

Basically speaking, soils can be classed as clay, sand, or something between the two. The nature of a particular soil depends on the size of its individual particles. Clay, for example, is composed of minute, flattened grains that group together very tightly, producing a compact, "heavy" soil that is difficult for plant roots to penetrate. The pore spaces are microscopic; water drains through them very slowly, and air space is extremely limited.

Sandy soils contain the largest particles of any soil—more than 25 times the size of the largest clay grains—and have correspondingly large pore spaces. This type of soil drains well (and is thus well aerated), but retains moisture and dissolved nutrients so poorly that plants need more frequent attention than they do when planted in clay.

Loam, the happy medium so often mentioned in garden books, may contain particles of intermediate size or a combination of particle sizes. In its drainage, aeration, and moisture retention, loam also represents a midpoint between the extremes of clay and sand.

How do you know what sort of soil you have? Appearance and texture can tell you a lot. Clay soils will usually crack when dry; sandy ones won't. When wet, clay may feel almost greasy; sand will feel gritty. Finally, if you dig a foot-deep hole, fill it with water, and still see water in it an hour later, your soil is probably on the clayey side (but see "Soil depth," below).

Soil depth

Once you've identified the basic type of soil in your garden, the next step is to determine its depth. With a spade or spading fork, dig a hole about 2 feet deep in the area where you want to plant. If you're lucky, you won't hit any obstructions—and neither will rose roots. It's possible, though, that you'll encounter complications: hardpan (a layer of impervious soil, usually found only in low-rainfall

Soil Particles & Soil Types

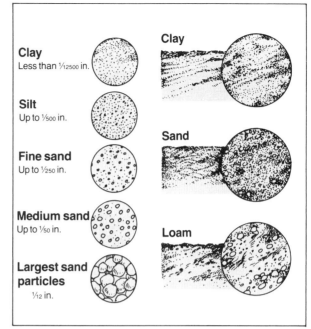

Size of mineral particles determines a soil's texture and type. Loam, combining organic and mineral particles of various sizes, is "ideal" garden soil.

regions), bedrock (or at least the parent material of your soil, such as limestone or sandstone), or occasional boulders too large to remove.

If the hardpan you run into is not too thick, you may be able to break through it, then laboriously but successfully remove it from a planting bed. The subsoil beneath it will often drain adequately. If you find a bedrock layer, though, you'll have to construct raised planting beds; the combination of native top soil and new soil added to the beds should provide the necessary 2-foot depth for your roses' roots. Immovable boulders, of course, are a problem that can't be solved; just choose another site.

Soil around new homes is sometimes severely compacted by the heavy equipment used in construction and may also contain quantities of building debris. In a light to medium soil, the situation can usually be remedied by deep digging (and the accompanying aeration) plus incorporation of organic matter. If you're faced with compacted clay, though, it may be easier and more effective simply to build raised beds as described on page 71.

Improving your soil

Organic matter—decomposing plant and animal remains—is good medicine for any soil; certain inorganic materials can also help.

Organic amendments. To put it simply, organic matter improves soil by lodging between soil particles and groups of particles. In clay, particles of organic matter act as wedges, separating the closely packed soil particles and thereby increasing drainage and aeration. In sandy soil, organic matter fills in the larger spaces between particles, allowing the soil to retain more water and dissolved nutrients.

The ongoing breakdown of organic matter by soil microorganisms produces *humus*, a gel-like substance that binds particles together into small units (often referred to as "crumbs"), producing the easy-to-dig condition so characteristic of soils high in organic matter.

The type of organic material you use to improve your garden will depend to some extent on when you add it— well in advance of planting or at the same time you set in your roses (see "When to prepare," below right). In either case, there's a wide range of choices. Easiest to find (but relatively expensive) are commercially packaged items such as peat moss, steer manure, redwood sawdust, alfalfa pellets, and leaf mold. Less costly (if you can haul them away yourself) are various animal manures and a number of locally produced agricultural by-products: grape or apple pomace, rice hulls, ground corncobs, wood products such as sawdust and shavings, mushroom compost, and spent hops, to name only a few. And if you maintain a compost heap, you need not search beyond your own back yard.

How much to add. Whatever organic material you use, the added amount should comprise about 25 percent by volume of the soil prepared: that is, if you're digging to a depth of 8 to 9 inches, you should incorporate about 3 inches of organic matter. (For easier work and more uniform results, dig in only a 2-inch layer of material at a time.)

Another point to keep in mind is that it's better to dig or till the materials into the *entire* planting area; roots will then be able to penetrate a fairly uniform soil as they grow. However, if your soil is sandy to sandy loam, you can safely add appropriate organic materials to the backfill soil at planting time; this will improve retention of water and nutrients in the rooting area. In a claylike soil, it's better to use just your basic garden soil as backfill. If you lighten the backfill, the soil in the planting hole will absorb water more rapidly and retain it longer than the surrounding clay, resulting in a waterlogged area around rose roots.

Inorganic amendments. Though organic matter is probably the primary soil amendment you'll use, several inorganic materials can also improve soil under certain conditions. Gypsum and lime have been used to open up some clay soils; both these products can cause the clay grains to cling together in larger "crumbs," thus improving drainage and workability. The choice between gypsum and lime depends on the soil's pH (see "Soil Testing," at left). Gypsum has been effective in certain Southwest soils rendered alkaline by a high sodium content; lime may be useful where soil is acid (generally in high-rainfall regions), since it also helps raise the pH toward neutral. Before using either product, check with your county agricultural agent.

Some rose growers add perlite—a hard, porous, granular, inert material derived from silica—to soil in containers, raised beds, and even individual planting holes. The perlite granules not only open a soil's structure, but also absorb and hold water and dissolved nutrients. Perlite is costly to use in quantity, but the effects are long lasting.

When to prepare. If you know several months in advance that you're going to plant roses, you can prepare soil early, giving it the chance to mellow and settle before planting time. This is also the time to add phosphorus and potassium fertilizers (see page 79). For autumn planting, prepare your soil in summer; if you want to plant in winter or spring, prepare in early autumn at the latest.

Advance preparation allows you a wider choice in organic amendments than can safely be used at planting time. For example, if you dig in fresh animal manures (which burn newly planted rose roots) and undecomposed organic matter (which takes nitrogen from the soil to aid its breakdown) a few months ahead, they'll mellow sufficiently by planting time to pose no dangers to your roses.

If you do choose to improve the soil at the time you plant new roses, be sure to use organic materials that contain enough nitrogen for their decomposition (such as nitrogen-fortified wood products), materials that are significantly decomposed (compost or leaf mold, for example), or peat moss, which breaks down so slowly that there is no significant nitrogen depletion. Unless you're sure it's thoroughly aged, don't risk using animal manure where it would come into direct contact with roots.

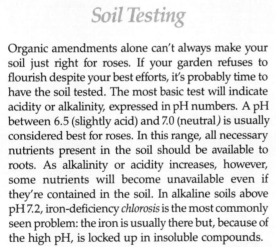

Soil Testing

Organic amendments alone can't always make your soil just right for roses. If your garden refuses to flourish despite your best efforts, it's probably time to have the soil tested. The most basic test will indicate acidity or alkalinity, expressed in pH numbers. A pH between 6.5 (slightly acid) and 7.0 (neutral) is usually considered best for roses. In this range, all necessary nutrients present in the soil should be available to roots. As alkalinity or acidity increases, however, some nutrients will become unavailable even if they're contained in the soil. In alkaline soils above pH 7.2, iron-deficiency *chlorosis* is the most commonly seen problem: the iron is usually there but, because of the high pH, is locked up in insoluble compounds.

You can buy soil-testing kits or arrange for testing by your county department of agriculture, state university, or a private soil-testing agency. Professionally conducted tests will give you the most detailed analyses and may be accompanied by recommendations for correcting any problems. Regardless of who conducts the test, be sure you obtain the soil sample exactly as directed; otherwise, the results may be meaningless.

A final tip for growers in cold-winter regions: mulching the prepared soil before the first frost will keep it workable after uncovered ground is frozen, making it possible to plant late-arriving bare-root roses.

Planting in problem sites

If your soil is simply too shallow for good root growth, or if it has drainage problems that cannot be remedied just by adding organic matter, you'll need to take some extra steps to improve drainage. Special procedures are also necessary to ensure good drainage in sloping plantings.

Raised beds. If your garden is level, a raised bed is the best solution to a severe drainage problem: water will easily percolate through the elevated soil in which you'll plant your roses. Plan to have the soil surface of the raised bed a minimum of 1 foot above the normal grade. Dig organic materials into the top 2 feet of native soil; then add additional soil to raise the bed and dig it (along with more organic matter) into the native soil beneath. Let the bed

settle for 2 months or so before you plant it. If settling is too great, mix more new soil into that in the bed.

Tile-drained beds. Where soil is poorly drained and the garden is on a slope (or if land near the proposed planting site slopes away from it), you can plant at ground level if you install drainage pipes or tile beneath the beds. After the pipes are in place, prepare the soil above them with organic materials; then let the beds settle before planting. When water passes down through the carefully prepared soil of the beds, it will enter the pipes and move out of the bed either by draining downslope or into a sump.

Terraced beds. Terraced plantings offer a neat solution to the problem of sharply sloping garden beds. The terraces provide a level planting surface, yet water will drain away down the slope. Wood, concrete blocks, brick, or even stone all make fine retaining walls for terraced beds. Regardless of the building material used, it's wise to incorporate several "weep holes" at the base of each wall; these allow excess water to drain easily out of the bed instead of collecting at the lowest part and building up pressure against the wall.

Planting Remedies for Problem Sites

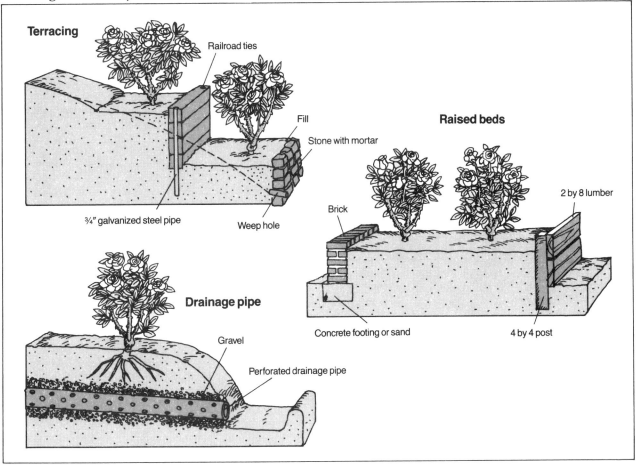

Problem situations don't have to rule out roses. A steep site can be terraced for rose planting; poorly drained soil can be dealt with by installing underground porous pipe or planting in raised beds.

Planting—Preparations & Procedures

Before you even pick up a shovel, examine your new bushes carefully. They should measure up to the grade advertised by the seller (see page 66) and should look robust, not weak or spindly. Root damage, if any, should be slight; if you do see injured roots, cut them back with a sharp, clean pair of pruning shears before you plant.

Occasionally, plants shipped during severe winter weather are frozen in transit. Freezing breaks up the cell structure of the canes and usually turns the roots black. Even if you thaw these plants carefully, they're practically worthless and should be replaced. Plants that have been overheated in transit will have live roots but black canes. Very rarely will you receive a diseased or dead plant.

Whenever the quality of the roses you receive does not meet your expectations, get in touch immediately with the nursery or mail-order specialist about possible replacement. Reputable sources are often happy to replace plants for you, even if the damage suffered was beyond their control.

Holding methods for plants

Weather and soil conditions permitting, the ideal time to plant new roses is the day you get them. If you cannot plant right away, you'll need to keep the new arrivals in a fresh but dormant condition until you're ready to set them out.

■ Heeling-in is the easiest way to hold new roses over a period of time. If you're dealing with just a few plants, group them together in a large container (a 5-gallon plastic or metal nursery can, for example) and "plant" them in a loose, moisture-retentive material such as sawdust, damp peat moss, perlite, or the like. Thoroughly water the material to settle it in around the roots; then place the container in a garage, basement, or other cool (but not freezing), dark place protected from drying wind.

Larger numbers of plants can be heeled-in directly in the ground—assuming, of course, that you can work the soil. In a shaded place, dig a trench with one slanted side. Lay the plants against the slant with their roots at the trench bottom, then cover both roots and canes with soil and thoroughly water them in. In these cool, shady conditions, the roses will take longer to break dormancy than they would if exposed to warming sunlight.

Whether they're held indoors or out, heeled-in roses should be planted at the very first opportunity. Root growth may begin while the plants are heeled-in—and the fewer roots there are to disturb during planting, the better.

■ Some roses are sold completely encased in plastic bags or sheets that do a good job of keeping the roots and canes moist. If you leave the unopened bags in a cool, dark place, the plants will hold safely for 7 to 10 days. If you must store the roses in warmer indoor conditions, be sure to unwrap the canes; otherwise, moisture will condense inside the plastic, turning the package into a miniature greenhouse and causing growth to begin.

Whatever holding method you use, *don't let the rose roots dry out*, even for a short time. Add water as needed to heeled-in roses; if you notice that plastic-wrapped plants have begun to grow, pack moist peat moss, sawdust, or other moisture-holding material around the roots.

Planting a Bare-root Rose

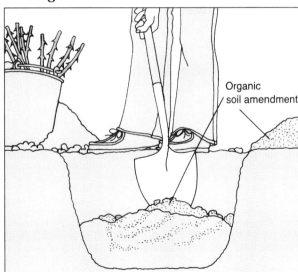

Dig planting hole large enough to hold rose roots without crowding or bending. In sand to sandy loam soils, you can mix soil amendments into backfill.

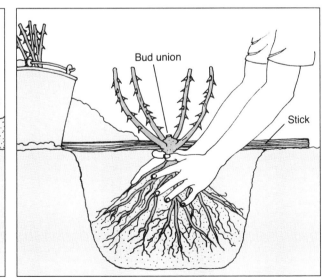

Form a firm cone of soil in hole, spread roots over cone. A stick placed across hole shows level of surrounding soil, lets you position bud union accurately.

Before you plant any bare-root rose bush, it's a good idea to soak the entire plant in water for 12 to 24 hours; this helps restore moisture to all the plant tissues at once. Some growers soak the plants in *muddy* water: the thin film of mud that adheres to the roots prevents them from drying out at all during the planting.

After you plant, mound damp soil or other moisture-retentive material over the lower parts of the canes to keep them from drying out while the roots are getting established. As new growth begins, gradually and carefully remove the mounded soil.

When to do bare-root planting

Technically, you can plant bare-root roses at any time during the dormant season when soil is not frozen. In much of the South and Southwest and on the West Coast, bare-root plants are most widely available in January and February; in some areas, planting can extend into March before plants break dormancy. Late autumn planting is also successful if you can get bare-root plants at that time; mail-order suppliers in cold-winter regions usually can ship rose plants as early as November. In general, if the winter lows in your region seldom reach 10°F/–12°C, the sooner you plant, the better.

In parts of the country where winter cold is capricious—alternating with spells of warmer weather—and where freezing typically settles in for several months, you will probably prefer (or be compelled) to plant in either autumn or spring. The one advantage to autumn planting is that new plants may have about a 5-month lead over spring-planted bushes in establishing their roots. In severe winters, though, little if any root growth will take place, and you do run the risk of losing even well-protected new plants. A premature warm spell may be just enough to break a new plant's dormancy, leaving it vulnerable to subsequent freezes. In contrast, spring planting has just one drawback: top growth and root growth begin almost simultaneously. If early spring weather is unseasonably warm, the top may temporarily outstrip the roots. In this case, you'll need to be very sure that roots always have enough water so that new growth won't wilt.

In cold-winter areas, the best advice on planting time will come from experienced local rose growers: friends, a reliable nurseryman who deals in roses, or the nearest Consulting Rosarian (see page 10). If you're a novice rose grower ordering from a large specialist nursery that has cold-storage facilities, you'd be wise to order for early spring planting; the grower can hold the new bushes over the winter under ideal conditions.

Bare-root planting steps

Over the years, no aspect of bare-root rose planting has aroused more controversy than the question of how high or low to position the bud union. For years, cold-winter rosarians set the bud union 1 to 2 inches below the soil surface to ensure winter insulation. Mild-climate growers, in contrast, positioned the bud union even with the soil surface or an inch or so above it, claiming that more new canes were produced when the bud union was exposed to sunlight.

Though some successful growers in cold-winter regions still plant roses with the bud union just below the soil surface, current thought favors setting bud unions even

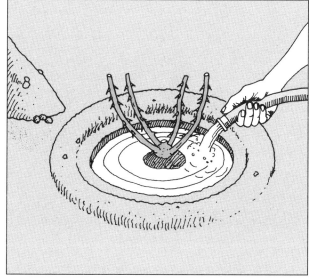

Fill soil in around roots, firming it with your hands or a stick as you go. Then thoroughly water rose, making sure it doesn't settle below established level.

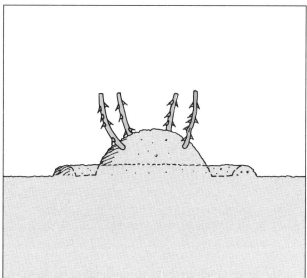

Mound moist soil over bud union and lower part of canes to prevent desiccation. Keep mound moist until new growth begins, then carefully remove soil.

♦ Planting

with the surface in all climates, carefully applying winter protection (see pages 90 to 91) if necessary. This positioning allows for good growth from the plant's base and, in time, may encourage roots to form from the bud union as well.

When planting own-root roses that have no bud union, place the juncture of roots and stems just below the soil surface.

Planting from containers

During the growing season, nurseries offer roses growing in fiber pots and in metal or plastic cans. Husky plants in large 3- to 5-gallon-size containers can provide good instant color, either to fill gaps in an existing planting or to create an entirely new rose garden.

If the plant is growing in a straight-sided metal can, you may want to have the can sides slit at the nursery to ease removal of the root ball. If you can't plant right away, water the slit-open container carefully to avoid washing out too much soil. Plants in plastic containers and taper-sided metal cans are simple to remove: just tap the container sides and bottom to loosen the root ball, then slide out the plant. This technique works with fiber pots as well, though it may be just as easy to tear the fiber from the root ball.

Dig each planting hole as shown in the illustrations at right. The central plateau of firm soil keeps the root ball from sinking—and ending up too deep in the hole—after planting. If the roots are coiled, gently loosen them and spread them out into the hole; otherwise, leave the root ball intact. Fill in soil around the root ball until the hole is about half-full, then water it in; fill in the remaining soil and water again. If the plant has settled, raise it gently now, while the soil is still saturated.

Miniature roses

"Miniature" is a relative term: not all miniature roses are the same dwarf size. When planted in the ground, some types remain under a foot high in even the best of conditions, while others may grow into shrubs 3 feet tall or taller. If you want plants of a uniform size—in a hedge or border, for example—it's best to plant just one variety or to choose varieties you've seen growing side by side in the ground under the same conditions.

Among container-grown minis, size differences among types are less pronounced—but you'll still notice that some kinds have distinctly larger flowers, leaves, and canes.

In contrast to nearly all other modern roses sold, bush and climbing miniatures are grown on their own roots (miniature standards are budded onto an understock trunk). Plants purchased locally will be in small pots; mail-

Planting from a Container

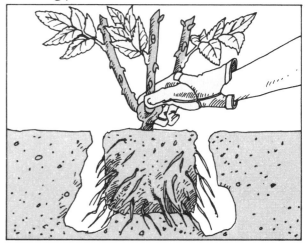

So that roots can penetrate soil more easily, dig hole wider at bottom and leave sides rough. A firm "plateau" beneath root ball keeps plant from settling.

After you position plant, fill in soil around root ball, then water thoroughly; adjust plant level if settling occurs. Ring of soil around plant forms watering basin.

order plants usually come in pots or with the root balls intact and wrapped in a moisture-retentive material. Plants purchased by mail may have yellowed or drooping leaves when they arrive at your door, but they'll revive if soaked overnight in water.

Miniatures outdoors. In their soil requirements and need for sunshine, miniatures are no different from other roses. There is one important planting difference, though: miniatures should be set *slightly* lower than they were in their nursery containers to encourage more root formation. Also keep in mind that newly planted small miniatures are easily stressed by drying winds and hot sunshine until their roots are well settled into their new quarters. For the first week or two, shelter new plantings from the elements; if the air is dry, sprinkle the foliage often.

Miniatures have extensive but rather shallow root systems, so a temporary drought imposed by a neglectful gardener is much more critical to these plants than to their larger and deeper-rooted brethren. Keep the soil constantly moist, but not soggy, and use a mulch to help conserve moisture (see page 77).

Miniatures in containers. Indoor miniatures (see below) will always be potted, of course, but you might also enjoy container-grown miniatures arrayed on a low wall or garden shelf outdoors. In either case, an 8-inch pot is a good beginning for most new bushes, though miniature standards may need a 10- to 12-inch pot or tub at first. Any container you use should have drainage holes and a depth of at least 6 inches. For the soil mix, use equal parts of good garden soil, organic matter (such as peat moss), and perlite.

Container-grown miniatures need attentive, thorough watering. To ensure that the soil is moist all the way through, and to flush out any potentially harmful salts, always water until the container begins to drain from the bottom.

Miniatures indoors. Temperature, humidity, and light are the three factors that most influence success with miniatures indoors. Choose a room that's about 70° to 75°F/21° to 24°C during the day, 60° to 65°F/16° to 18°C at night. Set the plants near a window with good light, but make sure they're not in hot, direct sun. Don't put them on a narrow window sill: they could be burned by sun through the glass, then chilled by the night air. If you have no well-lighted window space, you can provide adequate indoor illumination with fluorescent lights, particularly those designed for indoor plant growth. For best performance, suspend two tubes with a reflector 10 to 14 inches above the plants.

The dry atmosphere of the average home is too arid for the liking of miniature roses. To provide more humidity, set the pots on trays of gravel, then fill the trays with water up to the pot bases; as it evaporates, the water will humidify the surrounding air. Always keep plants away from heaters.

Give indoor miniature roses liquid fertilizer (see page 80) every 3 to 4 weeks. Pest or disease control (see pages 82 to 85) may be called for from time to time; spider mites, in particular, seem to relish indoor miniatures. When you need to dust or spray, do so outdoors.

Roses in containers

Blooming roses in containers are a possibility in any part of the country. They offer a lovely adornment for patio, deck or terrace—and where winters are severe, cold protection is simplified, since plants can be moved without disturbing the roots to a sheltered porch, garage, or basement. But before you decide to establish a full-scale container rose garden, realize that any pot-grown plant is going to require more attention to the routine culture essentials.

Choosing a container. Because they offer more root room than pots or round, tapered tubs, straight-sided wooden boxes are the best containers for roses. Nurseries, garden supply shops, and mail-order houses all sell square or rectangular boxes in various sizes, and if you're a handy carpenter, you can even make your own. In any case, be sure your planters are made from decay-resistant wood: redwood, cedar, or cypress. It's also important not to skimp on size. A 14-inch-square box is about the smallest you'll want to use for polyanthas and smaller floribundas, while hybrid teas and the more robust floribundas will be better off in 16- to 20-inch boxes. For any container, about a 16-inch depth is minimum.

Once filled with soil, any planter box will be quite heavy. If you plan to move your container-grown roses from one place to another, attach casters to the bottoms or put each box on a platform with casters. In the latter case, make sure the platform has drainage holes that line up with those in the container.

Soil & care. Container-grown roses need a well-drained, noncompacting medium, most easily achieved by mixing your garden soil with organic materials such as peat moss or any of the commercially packaged planting mixes. If your topsoil is on the heavy (clay) side, use a mixture of half garden soil to half organic material; for lighter soils, you can use a greater percentage of soil—about two parts to one of organic material.

After you cover the bottom of the container with prepared planting mixture, set the bare-root plant inside. You may have to bend the roots slightly to fit them into the container, but if they're so long that you must coil them around the bottom, cut off the part that coils. Center the plant, spread out the roots, and fill in around them with the prepared soil, firming it well with your fingers around the roots and under the crown. When you are finished planting, the bud union should be about 1 inch above the soil; the soil surface should be about 2 inches below the container's rim.

After firming the plant in, water it until the soil is thoroughly saturated and water runs out the drainage holes. If the soil settles too much, continue to add more soil and water it until the level remains 2 inches below the container rim. If the rose itself has also settled, return it to its proper depth by jiggling it from side to side while pulling upward on the shank between roots and bud union. To avoid tearing or breaking roots, do this while the planting soil is flooded.

After growth begins, water often enough to keep soil moist but not soggy. Never let the soil get so dry that the plant droops.

Like roses grown in the ground, tubbed bushes perform best when their roots are cool. This is sometimes difficult to achieve in containers; it helps to use good-size boxes, water frequently, and locate your roses where containers (but not plants) are shaded. Another way to moderate soil temperature (especially effective for miniatures) is to nest the container inside another one that's at least an inch bigger all the way around, then fill the space between the two with vermiculite. If you keep the vermiculite moist, it will insulate the soil and keep the temperature down.

Watering

The rose is a thirsty plant. Though the bushes will usually survive on skimpy watering, they'll perform at their vigorous best only when their roots are kept moist during the growing season. Even in regions where spring and summer rainfall is frequent, you may well need to augment the natural water supply to satisfy your roses' needs.

How much & how often?

A frequently quoted rule of thumb is that roses need at least 1 inch of rainfall, or its equivalent, per week. More precisely, they need water to the full depth of their roots—a penetration of 16 to 18 inches—in enough quantity to keep the soil constantly moist, yet never saturated for any length of time. Frequent but light waterings are neither sufficient nor desirable: if only the upper few inches of soil are kept moist, a network of feeder roots will grow just beneath the surface, where they may be burned by fertilizers, injured by cultivating or weeding, or damaged if the surface soil layer dries out.

To determine just how much water to give your roses, you need to consider your soil type (see page 69). According to studies performed by the University of California, 1 cubic inch of water on top of the ground will wet directly downward 1 foot in sandy soil, 6 to 10 inches in loam, or 4 to 5 inches in clay. To put it another way, to wet the soil to a 2-foot depth in a 2-foot-square basin requires 5 gallons of water in sandy soil, 7.6 gallons in loam, and 13.2 gallons in clay. Few people would want to take the time to water their roses by the gallon, but these figures point out that a trickle from the hose will take longer to produce the necessary penetration in clay soil than in sand.

How can you tell if your watering has penetrated deeply enough? The surest way is to conduct a simple test. Begin by watering your roses as you normally would—or pick an arbitrary amount of time (say, 15 minutes). The day after you water, dig down about 1½ feet to see how far your watering actually penetrated. If you discover, for example, that 30 minutes of irrigation wet only the top 10 inches of soil, you'll know that longer watering is needed to moisten the entire root zone.

Besides finding out how *much* water your roses need, you'll also need to learn how *often* to water them. Here again, the answer depends on your soil. Sandy soils absorb water rapidly, but also dry out quickly; clays take up water slowly, but retain it longer than sand. In sandy soil, then, you will spend fewer hours at a time watering your roses than you would in clay, but you'll return to do it more often. For example, during "average" spring weather, you may have to water your roses about every 5 days in sand, every 7 to 10 days in loam, but only every other week in clay. Do keep in mind that other factors besides soil types will also affect watering frequency: amount of rainfall, the presence or absence of a mulch (see facing page), wind, daytime temperatures, and amount of sunlight.

If you live in a summer-rainfall region, a rain gauge placed in the rose garden—out of reach of any sprinklers—will give you a fairly accurate (and perhaps surprising) record of how much water Nature is providing. But the easiest way to check the need for water is simply to dig a small hole in your rose bed, then feel with your finger to see if the earth is still moist (not soggy) 3 inches below the surface. If it's damp, hold off on watering; if it's dry, water again for the usual amount of time.

Finally, don't overlook watering during the dormant season. Even though your roses are standing still, continue to water them on a limited schedule as long as the soil is not frozen.

How to apply water

When it comes to *how* to water your roses, you have a choice between irrigating and sprinkling. In summer-rainfall regions, most rosarians vote for some form of irrigation—rain washes foliage often enough, but it may not be sufficient to keep roots moist. Where summers are dry, regular irrigation augmented by periodic sprinkling of the entire garden is often the preferred system.

Particularly if you live in a smoggy or dusty area, you will do your plants a great favor by washing off their leaves every week or so. Besides removing dust, this "shower" will wash away some insect pests, notably aphids and spider mites. Do the job early in the morning of what promises to be a sunny day, so the leaves will be dry by nightfall.

Sprinkling. If you want to set up a sprinkler system, one of your first steps will be choosing the best sprinkler heads for the job. There's a wide assortment: lawn-type heads that deliver full-circle to fraction-of-a-circle coverage, rotating impact sprinklers that cover a great area from one head, oscillating kinds that send a rainfall-like spray high and wide. All of these can be used as hose-end sprinklers and moved around as needed, and may also fit nicely into a permanent, rigid-pipe system. Your selection will depend upon garden layout, your water pressure and delivery rate, and, to some extent, basic preference.

In order to provide even coverage for an entire rose planting, you'll need to determine the sprinkler's dispersal pattern. Place straight-sided cans of the same size at about 3-foot intervals in a straight line from the sprinkler head to the extent of its coverage; run the water for 30 minutes or so, then measure the water depth in each can. Then space your sprinkler heads so the overlaps will compensate for any uneven delivery.

Once you've ascertained the correct spacing for heads, you'll need to check the sprinkler's delivery capacity (in gallons per hour—gph—at a specified pressure) as well as your water system's pressure and its delivery capacity at that pressure. From this information, you can calculate the number of heads you'll be able to use at the same time and still achieve full coverage.

Basically, a mulch is any material you spread over the soil beneath your rose bushes—be it grass clippings, crushed rock, or any of a dozen other choices. But whatever mulch you choose, its primary function is to retard evaporation from the soil, thus keeping your roses' roots constantly moist. At the same time, simply by presenting a barrier to the sun's rays, a mulch keeps the soil evenly cool—and protects feeder roots near the surface from harmful temperature fluctuations. (Remember, though, that the soil should not be so cool that it slows root growth. Where soil temperatures remain below freezing for much of the winter, delay mulching in spring until the soil has warmed up.)

Generally, a mulch an inch or two thick also serves as an effective weed control agent; any weeds that come up in the mulch can be pulled easily.

If you use an organic mulch, it will eventually decompose, and therein lies a further benefit: such decomposition improves the soil near the surface, making it looser, better draining, and easier for roots to penetrate.

Mulch choices. There's no lack of choices for mulching your rose garden. Countless regionally produced "waste" materials are suitable; besides manures and wood by-products, you'll find crushed sugar cane residue *(bagasse)*, cotton seed hulls, ground corncobs, spent mushroom compost, apple or grape pomace, pine needles, and decomposed materials from the forest floor. And of course, you can opt for an inorganic mulch if you prefer.

When deciding on a mulch, consider how quickly the material decomposes and how it behaves when spread in a layer. Materials that break down rapidly (manures, sawdust or wood shavings, compost) will help improve the soil most quickly. But some of these (notably wood by-products) need nitrogen to aid their decomposition; if they're not nitrogen fortified, they'll take what they need from the soil, and your roses may suffer a deficiency. A *light* sprinkling of high-nitrogen fertilizer should prevent such nitrogen-competition problems. Manure, of course, is the classic example of a relatively fast-decomposing material that contains sufficient nitrogen for its own breakdown.

Some materials, such as lawn clippings and thin leaves, mat down so tightly that they prevent air and water from entering the soil. You can use lawn clippings, though—just apply them in a thin layer, then let that dry before adding fresh clippings.

Cocoa bean hulls and and other hard, crushed materials are long lasting, but do the least to improve the soil. Rock will also absorb great amounts of heat, then radiate it up underneath the foliage; this amounts to a hotfoot for roses where summers are warm and dry.

Probably the trickiest material to use as a mulch—and therefore one to avoid—is peat moss. It dries out quickly after the original wetting and, if allowed to dry completely, becomes almost waterproof.

When applying any mulch, don't pile it up on the base of the canes; spread it to within about an inch of the base of each rose.

Irrigation. Many rose growers, especially those living in arid regions, prefer to flood-irrigate their plants. This method allows deep watering without the evaporative loss inherent in sprinkling.

Though some gardeners like to link all their rose bushes with an elaborate system of canals, it's usually best to give each plant an individual basin—that way, irrigation water can be concentrated in the plant's root zone. The basic basin is simply a 2- to 6-inch-tall earthen dike extending around each plant. It should be 20 inches or more across, wide enough to encircle the bush just beyond the drip line. For established plantings, bring in soil from another part of the garden to make the basin ridges; don't scrape up soil from the rose bed, since you might accidentally damage some of the feeder roots lying just beneath the surface.

If you think a rose planting will be unattractive with each bush growing out of a separate craterlike basin, try spreading a mulch inside the basins and on the ground between as camouflage. Gardeners in arid regions where flood irrigation is employed for all plants often entirely surround their rose beds with a concrete curbing to contain the water.

Watering roses in basins presents a very minor efficiency problem. If you have just a few bushes, it's simplest to move the hose from plant to plant until all are watered. You can reduce the time this takes by employing one or more "Y" connections at the end of your principal hose, with secondary hoses going to more than one bush at a time. To avoid having soil scoured by water from the hose end, you can buy a "bubbler" attachment that diffuses the water through many small holes to reduce its force without cutting down the volume. An old sock or garden glove tied over the hose end accomplishes the same purpose.

To water many bushes at once (or even a few, if you don't want to bother with moving a hose), you can easily put together a watering system from plastic pipe or tubing and a fitting that connects your garden hose to the system. Rigid plastic (PVC) pipe is one material you might use: the

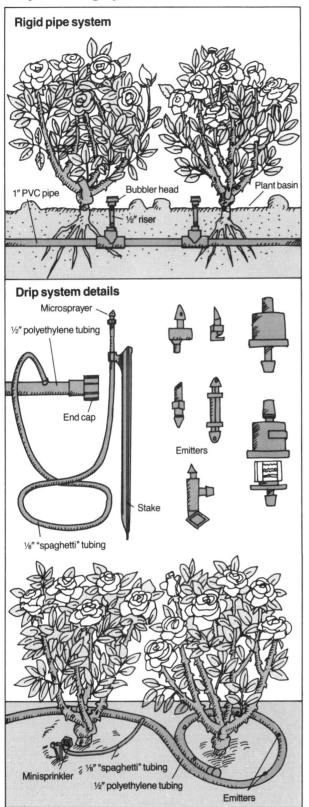

Rigid pipe system

1″ PVC pipe Bubbler head Plant basin

½″ riser

Drip system details

Microsprayer

½″ polyethylene tubing

End cap

Emitters

Stake

⅛″ "spaghetti" tubing

Minisprinkler ⅛″ "spaghetti" tubing

½″ polyethylene tubing

Emitters

Efficient watering systems can be made either from rigid plastic pipe and individual bubbler heads (above) or from plastic tubing and drip-irrigation hardware (below).

◆ *Watering*

drawing on this page shows a sample system. You cut the pipe with a saw and make all connections with plastic fittings and special glue or metal clamps, depending upon the type of pipe. Such rigid systems can be buried beneath a few inches of soil, though the openings for water emission must remain above ground.

Far easier to work with than plastic pipe is the flexible black, ½-inch polyethylene tubing used for drip irrigation (see below). You can cut it with pruning shears and make quick connections with specially made parts; and because the tubing is so flexible, you can lay it out in curves that follow your planting patterns. This sort of tubing was designed to rest on the soil surface, where it can easily be obscured by mulch—but it, like rigid pipe, can be shallowly buried if you prefer.

Wherever winter temperatures fall low enough to freeze water in pipes or tubing, be sure to drain systems completely in autumn.

Drip irrigation. Simply described, drip irrigation concentrates delivery of water in a plant's root zone, using special slow-delivery emitters that allow you to water a great number of plants at one time. The foundation of the system is flexible polyethylene tubing about ½ inch in diameter; special plastic fittings let you make normal pipe-fitting-type connections. The low-volume emitters you need can attach directly to the main tubing or can be positioned at some length from it, connected by ⅛-inch microtubing ("spaghetti" tubing). Emitter choices include microsprayers, minisprinklers, and drip or trickle devices; delivery rates range from ½ gallon to over 20 gallons per hour. A visit to a good supplier will acquaint you with all the possibilities.

Compared to traditional watering methods, drip systems take longer to achieve the needed depth of penetration. In their favor, though, is their great adaptability. The system can be hooked up to the main water line (after you connect an antisiphon valve and pressure regulator) or simply attached to a hose or hose bibb. You can arrange the tubing to water an entire bed of roses or lay it out to deliver water to widely separated bushes simultaneously; you can set up inconspicuous systems that will water all the pots in an extensive container garden. Drip irrigation systems can be operated by controllers (see below), and they'll easily deliver a fertilizer solution if equipped with one of the fertilizer injectors mentioned on page 80.

Controllers. If your planting is served by some sort of water-delivery system, you can arrange to water it automatically. All you need do is connect an electronic controller ("timer") to the system. Controllers can be programmed to a variety of frequencies and durations of waterings, so your roses can be watered whether you're home or away. Most controllers operate on standard 110-volt household electricity, though you can buy battery-powered models that will control a system far from convenient electrical supply.

Fertilizing

If a rose isn't fertilized, it won't necessarily dwindle away: many species and shrub roses will flourish without any supplemental nutrients at all. But virtually all modern roses and most of the old garden types need a little assistance to turn in a peak performance.

The major nutrients

Like most familiar garden plants, roses must have three basic nutrients for healthy growth: nitrogen, phosphorus, and potassium.

Nitrogen. When properly applied (see page 80) to plants receiving adequate water, nitrogen produces faster effects than any other nutrient: increased volume of growth, deeper green color, greater leaf size, and more and better blooms. Roses that are performing halfheartedly or just sitting still may need only the tonic of a nitrogen fertilizer. Don't go overboard, though: too much nitrogen will stimulate vegetative growth at the expense of flower production, possibly resulting in lush leaves susceptible to disease and rangy, sappy growth that's easily damaged by cold. (You may also end up with a dead plant—a casualty of fertilizer-burned roots.)

Nitrogen is available to plants only from compounds it forms with other elements, and then only in its *nitrate* form. If applied as *ammonia* or *nitrite*—as in organic fertilizers such as bloodmeal—nitrogen must usually be converted to nitrate in the soil before plants can use it. Because nitrate is so readily soluble, whatever is not taken up by roots soon after application will be leached from the root zone by rain or routine deep watering (leaching is especially rapid in sandy soil). For this reason, many rose gardeners prefer fertilizers offering a slow, sustained release of nitrogen; choose one that derives all or part of its nitrogen from urea (or urea-form), or use a controlled-release type.

Phosphorus. This element is crucial for early root development; it also plays a vital role in flower formation, seed production, and, later on, the maturation of a plant's growth. A phosphorus deficiency may be revealed in stunted growth and browned leaf tips on a plant with fewer flowers than normal.

Manufactured fertilizers contain phosphorus as phosphoric acid (P_2O_5). Unlike nitrate, phosphoric acid doesn't dissolve readily; instead, it binds to mineral particles in the top 1 to 2 inches of soil, then slowly releases elemental phosphorus to nearby plant roots. Thus, surface applications of phosphorus only benefit *surface* roots; to reach your roses' entire root zone, you'll have to dig fertilizer into the soil before planting time.

Most soils contain adequate phosphorus. In definitely acid soils, though, it may be locked up in insoluble compounds. Raising the soil's pH to the range suitable for roses (see "Soil Testing," page 70) should release some or much of these reserves.

Potassium. Like nitrogen and phosphorus, potassium is not available to plants in its elemental form. It's always applied in the compound potassium oxide (K_2O), usually referred to as "potash." Like phosphorus, the soluble potash in fertilizers does not leach down through the soil but, instead, becomes part of the exchangeable potassium in the upper few inches. To supply potassium deep in the root zone—where it will do plants the most good—you'll need to add it to the soil before planting.

Potassium deficiency—signaled by slow growth and browned leaf margins—is less common than low levels of nitrogen or phosphorus. The problem most typically occurs in lighter, sandier soils and in highly organic "peat" soils.

Secondary nutrients & trace elements

Because plants need calcium, magnesium, and sulfur in far smaller amounts than they do nitrogen, phosphorus, and potassium, these nutrients are called "secondary." Most soils contain them in adequate supply, but it's worth noting that sulfur deficiency may occur in high-rainfall areas of the Pacific Northwest. In these regions, periodic sulfur application is needed to replace sulfur leached from the soil by heavy rains.

Seven other nutrients are referred to as "trace elements." Boron, chlorine, copper, iron, manganese, molybdenum, and zinc are all essential for proper plant development, but each is needed in only a very low quantity. *Chlorosis* is probably the most frequently encountered trace element deficiency; in plants lacking iron, leaves turn yellow while their veins remain green. The problem usually arises when iron, though not absent from the soil, is present in a form unavailable to plants. Chlorosis is most common in alkaline soils—and in fact, you'll typically find trace element deficiencies only in extremely acid or alkaline conditions. Adjusting the pH may be all that's required to restore an element's availability.

If you plan to add trace elements (other than iron) to your soil, do so cautiously—and preferably only after a thorough soil analysis. An excess of these elements can be just as detrimental as a deficiency.

Types of fertilizers

Whether you use inorganic or organic fertilizers (or both), you have a choice between two types: dry and liquid. In either case, follow the application and dosage instructions on the package carefully. *Never* assume that if a little fertilizer is good, more will be better: this can do more harm than good. If you're tempted to deviate from the recommendations, give your plants more frequent doses at a *lower* strength.

✦ Fertilizing

Dry fertilizers. Of all fertilizers, these are the most widely available and generally used.

Dry granular fertilizers constitute the bulk of dry fertilizers sold. Organic kinds include such products as bloodmeal and cottonseed meal; inorganics include a vast array of packaged types, ranging from single-element sorts (ammonium sulfate, for example) to a range of "complete" fertilizers such as "rose food," "vegetable food," and the like. Organic fertilizers release their nutrients as they are acted upon by soil microorganisms. The inorganics dissolve when water contacts them; how fast they dissolve (and hence, how long they last) depends upon the product.

To avoid any risk of burning plant roots, apply dry inorganic fertilizers only to moist soil. It's best to water your roses well the day before you plan to fertilize; the next day, *lightly* scratch the soil surface (no more than ½ inch deep) and scatter the recommended amount of fertilizer beneath the bush out to the edge of the foliage drip line, keeping it several inches away from the base of the plant. Finally, thoroughly soak in the fertilizer.

Controlled-release fertilizers are little pellets of dry fertilizer coated with a permeable resin. With each watering, some of the fertilizer dissolves and moves through the coating into the soil. Products differ in their nutrient formulas and in the length of time they remain effective: some last for 3 to 4 months with normal garden watering, some for 8 to 9 months or more. In any case, though, using controlled-release fertilizers usually means you won't need to fertilize your roses as often.

For roses growing in containers, controlled-release fertilizers can be especially appropriate, since they won't be leached out of the soil as rapidly as dry granular fertilizers. Nonetheless, because containers require such frequent watering, even controlled-release types may be used up more rapidly than is stated on the package.

Application of controlled-release fertilizers is simple: you just scratch the pellets into the soil until they're barely covered, then water them in.

Liquid fertilizers. These products are sold as liquid or dry concentrates which must be diluted or dissolved in water before application. Once in solution, nutrients are absorbed quickly and easily by plant roots, often producing noticeable results in a short time. You'll find an extensive choice of brands and formulas; most are inorganic, though one of the best-known types—fish emulsion—is organic.

Liquids are a great shot in the arm for neglected bushes and a fine supplement to a dry fertilizer program—and modern trends point to them as an increasingly popular regular (or even total) nutrient source. In fact, some growers who water their plantings by drip irrigation find it simplest to fertilize exclusively with liquids delivered through one of the devices described below.

If you grow only a few roses, you may be content to mix a fertilizer solution in a watering can and carry it from bush to bush (or container to container), preparing more solution as needed. But if your garden is more extensive, you might appreciate the convenience of a device that can inject fertilizer directly into your hose or watering system. The simplest of these gadgets is a siphon hose attachment. You mix a bucketful of concentrated fertilizer solution; the water flowing through the hose extracts a measured amount of the solution through the siphon and dilutes it to the proper strength in the water running from the hose. Another popular device is a small canister that attaches between hose bibb and hose. You put dry fertilizer powder or tablets in the canister; when water flows through it, it measures a precise amount of fertilizer into the hose or water line. For larger plantings, or whenever you want greater flexibility in fertilizer choice or concentration, you can install a fertilizer injector directly into the water line.

Foliar fertilizers. Since roses can assimilate nutrients through their leaves, spraying fertilizer solutions onto foliage can be a beneficial *supplement* to soil fertilization. Any liquid fertilizer will do the job, as long as the label specifies that it's safe for foliage. You simply spray the nutrient mixture on leaf undersides, just as you would an insecticide; from there, it's taken up through each leaf's breathing pores (stomata) and becomes almost immediately available for the plant's use. Add a spreader-sticker to the solution to ensure that the spray will adhere to the leaves; or, after you mix the fertilizer solution, add about ¼ teaspoon of a phosphate-free household dishwashing detergent to each gallon.

Many foliar fertilizers can be combined with some of the common insecticides and fungicides, letting you complete several jobs in a single pass through the garden. But don't guess—be sure all the chemicals are compatible. Check labels for any warnings; if you have questions, consult your County Cooperative Extension Advisor (or agricultural advisor) or a successful rose grower in your area.

To reap the full rewards of foliar fertilizing, establish a consistent program. Begin in spring when the first leaves have formed; continue every 2 to 3 weeks until midsummer in cold-winter regions or until about mid-September where winters are mild. One word of caution: foliar fertilizing may cause leaf burn in hot weather. As a rule of thumb, don't apply foliar fertilizers if the temperature is above 90°F/32°C.

When to apply fertilizer

Fertilizing guidelines differ a bit depending on the rose: in-ground bush or climber, miniature rose, or container-grown plant. In all cases, though, refrain from fertilizing new plants until they've completed one flowering cycle.

Roses in the ground. Fertilize first in early spring, soon after you finish pruning. Concerning later applications, there are two schools of thought. One approach advocates applying fertilizer just after each burst of bloom, thus supplying bushes with the nutrients they need for the next flower show. If you want to enter this on the calendar, you can figure that, for the average hybrid tea, the cycle of

Though you can apply some of the major and secondary nutrients individually, many rose growers—both novices and old pros—prefer the convenience of a good commercial fertilizer containing all three major elements in specific proportions.

Some of these balanced fertilizers, marketed as "rose food," are formulated to suit most rose-growing conditions throughout the country. Certain brands even contain systemic insecticides that remain effective for a month or so and can kill sucking insects.

On the label of any package of "complete" fertilizer, you'll find three numbers—10-5-5, for example—indicating the proportions of nitrogen, phosphorus, and potassium, in that order. Thus, a 10-5-5 fertilizer contains 10 percent nitrogen, 5 percent phosphoric acid, and 5 percent potash. The label also provides a "guaranteed analysis," telling you not only the percentages of all nutrients in the fertilizer, but also their sources.

If you want to compare fertilizers (to determine which is a better value, perhaps), you can easily compute "actual nitrogen" (or actual anything else): just multiply the stated percentage of the nutrient by the package weight. For example, a 10-pound bag of 20 percent nitrogen fertilizer contains 2 pounds of actual nitrogen.

Numbers on a fertilizer's label show the percentage of each major nutrient. The guaranteed analysis gives more detail, spelling out the source of each nutrient.

growth from the start of a flowering shoot to the opening of a bud covers 45 to 60 days.

The second, widely followed approach suggests fertilizing in smaller, regular doses, at 2-, 3-, or 4-week intervals. This theory holds that because nutrient need is continuous and because nitrogen in particular is so easily leached from the soil, one heavier application every 6 weeks may not provide enough for a plant throughout the entire period. Those who fertilize every 2 weeks usually alternate a dry fertilizer with a liquid soil or foliar fertilizer.

Actually, both approaches can work very well. The first method is easier simply because you fertilize less often; but if that is your choice, you will want to stick to the powdered or pelletized dry fertilizers that release their nutrients over a period of time. Gardeners with fast-draining soils usually get better results from more frequent fertilizing.

Even if you use a controlled-release fertilizer that will provide nutrients over half or more of the growing season, you may wish to give your roses additional nutrient boosts while they are actively growing. For this, a liquid fertilizer applied to either foliage or soil will provide supplementary nutrition in amounts you can regulate easily.

Fertilizing miniatures. Though miniatures are small, they still need fertilizer for best growth. After new bushes have produced their first crop of flowers, apply a liquid fertilizer every 3 to 4 weeks during the rest of the first season. In the second and subsequent years, you can give plants a dry complete fertilizer at the start of the growing season, then follow up throughout the season with the fertilizing program of your choice.

Fertilizing container plants. Because frequent and thorough watering continually leaches soluble nutrients from container soil mixtures, you'll want to fertilize container-grown roses regularly during the growing season. Liquid fertilizers are simple and safe to use in containers; you can regulate the concentration in each application, regardless of how much solution you apply. Should you prefer a dry fertilizer, apply it evenly, scratching it lightly into the soil; then water thoroughly. Many gardeners prefer a controlled-release type, since it lasts longer.

When to stop. Rose growers in regions where winter temperatures dip below about 10°F/–12°C have to consider when to *stop* fertilizing. Succulent new growth late in the season is likely to be ruined by fall frosts, and the plant that is still actively growing when freezing weather arrives is at a real disadvantage in getting through winter with little damage. Depending on how early the first damaging frost is expected, cold-climate rosarians give their last nitrogen applications anywhere from August 1 to early September—or no later than 6 weeks before anticipated freezing.

Common-sense Pest Control

Though they're often thought of as the delicate prima donnas of the garden, the truth is that roses are no more susceptible to pests and diseases than many other flowering shrubs. Much of the formidable-sounding pest-control advice you may have heard is geared toward rosarians who also raise their roses for show—and thus need plants unblemished in blossom, stem, and leaf. For the average gardener, though, a chewed or imperfect leaf here and there won't diminish a rose's beauty in the slightest.

Basic control

The first step in controlling pests and diseases is simply establishing good plant health. Constant application of chemical sprays won't turn a sickly rose into a thriving one if it has had to endure poor soil, insufficient water, lack of nutrients, or an unfavorable garden location or climate.

To keep your roses robust, begin with a thorough garden clean-up. Right after pruning, clear all leaves and other debris from beneath the bushes; before new growth emerges, give both plants and soil a thorough dormant spray (see "Pruning aftercare," page 89) to kill insect eggs and disease spores that have overwintered on soil, old leaves, or rose canes.

As the season progresses, check your roses often, and deal with problems as they arise. Remember, though, that your goal is *control*, not *elimination*. Experienced gardeners don't try to produce an antiseptic garden; they simply aim to limit potential pests and diseases to a level where they'll cause minimal plant damage.

For efficient control (with the least amount of work on your part), you'll want to keep the following points in mind:

■ Learn when each pest or disease is likely to appear. Insects and diseases come in cycles according to season and weather; it is senseless to employ remedies before a problem appears (certain foliage diseases excepted), or to continue using control methods after conditions that favor the problem have gone.

■ If you have a choice of several control materials, choose the least toxic one for trial. Some pests can even be controlled simply by washing them off foliage with a forceful spray of water. And many insects have natural enemies that can aid in control as long as you don't kill them, too.

■ Remember that a single application of a contact spray or a nontoxic control (see page 84) is usually ineffective in solving any pest or disease problem. A follow-up, generally within 7 to 10 days, will be needed to catch eggs or spores that hatch or germinate after the first treatment.

■ Read all instructions on spray labels carefully and follow them *exactly*. If for any reason you want to deviate from the directions, always seek advice. Check with your County Cooperative Extension Advisor (or agricultural advisor) or consult a successful rose grower in your area.

■ Many of the current insecticides are compatible with the standard fungicides, so you may be able to control both pests and diseases with one spray. Similarly, some foliar fertilizers may be combined with insect and disease control chemicals, allowing you to control and fertilize in one operation. *But before you mix any two products into one solution,* check product labels carefully for compatibility warnings.

Control options: dust or spray

For routine pest control, you can use spray or dust. Neither of these is categorically better than the other; your choice depends upon climatic conditions, how many roses you have, and, ultimately, how well the approach works for you.

Dusting. This method is easier in one respect: you do no mixing, but simply put the dust into an applicator and go to work. And when you're finished, there's no need to clean out the duster. Dusts don't generally provide as thorough coverage as sprays do, but thanks to the residue they leave on foliage, they're a bit longer lasting. Some people do object to the appearance of the dust residue, though; and where air pollution is a common problem, dusts further hamper transpiration from the leaves. Because of their washing action, sprays are preferable in such regions.

Though dusters vary in design (and in operating principles), all fall into two categories—continuous or intermittent flow. The continuous-flow sorts are the best (and the least tiring) to use on large or medium-size gardens. For a modest planting or just a few bushes, one of the intermittent-action types (bellows or plunger operated) does the job nicely; it also allows you a little better control of coverage, since you determine when the duster will emit its powder. Such dusters are excellent for small touch-up applications: you can even keep one loaded and ready to go at a moment's notice. Any duster should have a deflecting nozzle so that you can easily reach the undersides of leaves.

Do your dusting when the air is still, for even the slightest breeze tends to blow the dust everywhere but on the roses. Early mornings and evenings are usually the best times. And don't leave your roses looking as if you had dumped sacks of flour on them; a light, relatively inconspicuous coating is enough.

Spraying. Of the several points in favor of spraying, perhaps the most important is the wide variety of control materials available: from plain water and contact sprays to systemic insecticides and fungicides. A really fine spray mist lets you penetrate more deeply into the cracks and crevices of leaves and flowers than is possible with dusts.

The kind of sprayer you choose is largely determined by the number of bushes you have. With 100 bushes and a 1-gallon sprayer, filling and refilling the sprayer would take almost as much time as spraying the bushes. You're much

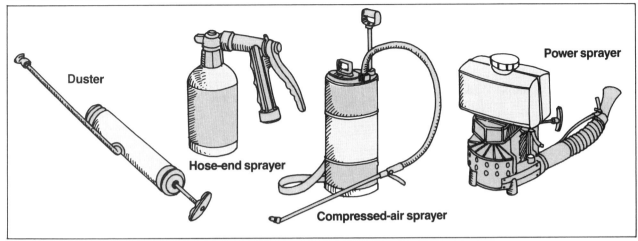

Dusting and spraying tools come in a range of styles and types, from hand-powered to motor-driven.

more likely to do the job as often as you should if you can finish the whole garden with a single batch of solution. No matter what sprayer you choose, however, it should be designed for easy coverage of the undersides of leaves.

Least expensive and simplest to prepare is the hose-attachment sprayer, a bottle and siphon arrangement that you attach to a garden hose which operates it by water pressure. You measure liquid spray concentrate into the bottle and dilute it with water according to instructions on the spray label. This solution is metered through a needle valve into the hose stream, where it is diluted to the proper concentration as it is discharged through a nozzle on the bottle cap. Offsetting ease of use, however, are several disadvantages. Hose-attachment sprayers are more wasteful of spray solution than the other sprayers mentioned below; consequently, they discharge a greater quantity of toxic material than is necessary for control. These sprayers also make it difficult to cover the undersides of leaves, especially those low on the plant. And if you fail to clean the siphon after each spraying, it may become coated with spray residue—resulting in improper dilution of spray material.

Compressed-air tank sprayers, available in capacities of 1 to 6 gallons, are suitable for both small and fairly large gardens. To use these sprayers, you measure the spray concentrate into the tank and dilute it with the required amount of water. Then you close the tank top and pump a plunger to get a high pressure for good coverage. As you spray, agitate the tank frequently to keep the solution mixed.

Because the larger compressed-air tanks are heavy and cumbersome when loaded, it's best to look for one with a wheel attachment—you can roll it rather than lug it. For freedom of movement among your roses, be sure to get the longest possible applicator hose; the hose should end in a tube bent at a 45° angle just before the spray head to allow for easy spraying under the leaves.

If you are a really ambitious grower with 200 or more plants to spray, you may find a gasoline or electric-powered tank sprayer a necessity. Operating at a maintained hose pressure of over 100 pounds, these tanks can throw a finely atomized spray with great force over a considerable area—actually giving greater coverage per gallon of solution than other sprayers. Using one of these, you can cover about 500 large bushes in 2 hours. Sizes range from 10 gallons on up; tanks usually are mounted on wheels.

Application tips. Applying a spray properly is as important as choosing the right controls and an efficient applicator. Whenever you use toxic pest control materials, remember the following points:

▪ Thoroughly cover both sides of the leaves. Begin at the base of each bush and work upward with a side-to-side rolling movement of the spray nozzle. Your objective is to cover the underside of every leaf, for this is the region most liable to insect and disease attack. By the time you reach the top of the bushes, most of the upper leaf surfaces will have been covered, too, by the "rainback" of your spray. If not, a quick spray over the tops should finish the job. Manufactured spreader-stickers, when added to a spray solution, will increase a spray's effectiveness by making it coat the leaves and adhere better. Even household detergent added to the solution (up to ¼ teaspoon to a gallon) will help.

▪ Spray when the air is still—in early morning (but after most of the dew has evaporated) or early evening. (In a humid-summer climate, morning spraying is better: you want the foliage to be dry by nightfall, to discourage mildew and other foliage diseases.) *Be very careful of any drift of your spray.* A number of pest control chemicals are toxic to wildlife, especially to honeybees and fish. Cover nearby fishponds and birdbaths while you spray; don't dump excess spray or wash spray equipment where the chemicals could run off into ponds or streams.

▪ To keep your sprayer in good working order and prolong its life, thoroughly clean it after each use.

◆ Pest Control

Plant problems & remedies

The insects and foliage diseases that may afflict your roses are discussed below; in the chart on the facing page, you'll find an illustration of each one and a list of possible remedies. These remedies are divided into three categories:

Nontoxic. Control is achieved by means other than a chemical poison.

Contact. The chemical control kills the insect or disease by surface contact.

Systemic. The toxic ingredient is absorbed into the plant; for a period of time following application, any sucking insect that ingests the plant's juices will be killed.

It should be stressed that the problems noted in the chart are *potential.* Though these pests and diseases *can* bother your roses, they're not guaranteed to show up in your garden; and even if they do, the infestation may not be significant enough to require control.

Pests. The following seven pests may cause problems for your roses.

Aphids can appear on new growth at any time during the growing season, but they're often most numerous on the first growth of spring. Natural enemies (ladybugs in particular) help keep aphids in check—a good reason for using nontoxic controls as your first resort.

Beetles of various sorts may do casual damage to leaves or flowers; if the pests are present only in small numbers, hand-picking is the simplest and safest control. Voracious Japanese beetles may require special controls in regions where they occur; consult your local agricultural advisor.

Borers are particularly frustrating because you don't discover their presence until they've done their damage—and then you have only hand-picking to rely on. Wilted new growth tips often indicate borer infestation, but not always—during warm to hot weather, new growth may wilt due to water stress but perk up again if the plant is watered.

Caterpillars and worms, the larvae of various flying insects, usually concentrate on rose foliage and immature buds. If infestation is light, hand-picking is simple: you'll usually find the pests near the damage you notice.

Mites are a warm-weather pest: the higher the temperature, the more rapidly they mature and the more eggs they lay. In time, an unchecked invasion can defoliate an entire plant. Mites are so small you can barely see them, but you can check for them in two ways. First, hold a piece of white paper beneath a leaf and tap the leaf; any mites will fall onto the paper, where you'll see them as little specks scurrying for cover. Second, if you have a magnifying glass, use it to check the leaf undersides. (Lower leaves usually are the first to be affected.)

A garden hose and water are the simplest weapons to use against mites. Using a nozzle that produces a fine spray,

thoroughly wash off the undersides of the leaves. Repeat this operation at least three times—either 3 days in a row or every other day for 6 days—to make sure of getting mites hatched from eggs already laid when you hosed off the leaves the first time.

If you use chemical miticides, be sure to spray at least two or three times, waiting as label specifies between sprayings. And because mites gain immunity to any one insecticide rather quickly, change miticides after several applications if you spray throughout a season.

Rose midge larvae drop to the soil after they've done their damage to new growth; there, they pupate and emerge in about a week as adult winged insects ready to begin a new generation. The soil is the critical area for control: you must kill adults as they emerge. Most effective is diazinon—either in granule form, sprinkled on the soil beneath the roses and for a distance of at least 6 feet beyond them, or in a spray applied to the same area. Follow-up applications may be needed if damage resumes later.

Thrips are especially vexing because they disfigure flower petals; roses in white and pastel shades are their favored targets. They appear with the onset of warm weather and increase in number as the season progresses. Thrips have a number of natural enemies, but serious infestations call for chemical controls. Always spray plants from *above,* making certain to cover all flowers and opening buds.

Diseases. Here are three diseases to look out for as you check your rose garden throughout the year.

Black spot, if not checked, can defoliate a plant at the height of the growing season. Bushes stripped of their leaves will fail to mature naturally—they'll continually try to produce new foliage to replace what was lost—and will thus be more susceptible to winter damage.

Black spot is common in regions with summer rainfall, since it spreads in water and thrives in warmth, but it has now moved into summer-dry areas as well, fostered by the water that roses require in such climates. The spores overwinter in lesions on canes and possibly on old leaves fallen to the ground. In spring, they germinate and reach new foliage via water from rainfall or sprinkling. Garden sanitation is your first line of defense: thoroughly clean up refuse at pruning time, then apply a dormant spray.

Powdery mildew is found virtually everywhere roses are grown. It flourishes in humid conditions, but unlike black spot, it does not spread in water—to become established, it needs dry leaves. Foggy coastal areas are ideal for its spread, as are overcrowded plantings in damp and shady gardens. Resistance varies from one rose variety to the next.

Rust usually makes its appearance in late spring and, if not controlled, can partially or completely defoliate a plant. As is true for black spot, garden sanitation is your first defense. Remove all old leaves from plants as well as from the ground at pruning time, then use a dormant spray. (In near-tropical areas such as Florida and Hawaii, where there is no completely dormant season, removal of all foliage is not a good idea. Use foliage sprays for control.)

PEST	DESCRIPTION	CONTROLS
Aphids	These soft-bodied, ⅛-inch-long insects may be green, red, brown, or black. They appear in early spring on new growth; if present in great numbers, they can slow growth, or stunt or deform leaves.	**Nontoxic:** water wash, spray with soap solution **Contact:** malathion, pyrethrins **Systemic:** disyston, Orthene
Beetles	Various beetles may visit roses. Many do little damage and are easily dealt with by hand-picking. Japanese beetles can be a problem in some regions; check with your county extension advisor.	**Nontoxic:** hand-pick **Contact:** diazinon, Mavrik, Sevin **Systemic:** none
Borers	These worms bore into new shoots and consume the stem's pith; suddenly wilting new growth tips provide the first indication of infestation. Hand-picking is the only control.	**Nontoxic:** hand-pick **Contact:** none **Systemic:** none
Caterpillars & worms	Collectively, this group includes various wormlike pests that skeletonize leaves or chew holes in them. Extent and severity of damage determine the need to control.	**Nontoxic:** hand-pick, *Bacillus thuringiensis* **Contact:** diazinon, Mavrik, Sevin **Systemic:** Orthene
Mites	These tiny pests do their damage by sucking juices from surface tissue, causing yellowed, dry-looking leaves that sometimes show silvery webbing underneath. Defoliation can result.	**Nontoxic:** water wash **Contact:** Avid, Mavrik, Plictran, Vendex **Systemic:** none
Rose midges	These near-microscopic pests (about ¹⁄₂₅ inch long) rasp tender tips of new growth, causing them to blacken and shrivel. The larvae pupate in soil, where control is effective.	**Nontoxic:** none **Contact:** diazinon **Systemic:** none
Thrips	Near-invisible insects that deform and discolor flower petals by rasping and puncturing tissues. They start in buds, working among unopened petals.	**Nontoxic:** none **Contact:** diazinon, Dursban, Mavrik, Thiodan **Systemic:** Cygon, Orthene

DISEASE	DESCRIPTION	CONTROLS
Black spot	This fungus disease causes black spots with irregular, fringed edges on leaves, sometimes stems; tissue around spots may turn yellow. Severe cases can result in defoliation.	**Nontoxic:** none **Contact:** folpet **Systemic:** benomyl, triforine
Powdery mildew	Gray to white, furry to powdery coating covers new growth of leaves, stems, and flower buds. Infected leaves become crumpled and distorted, and remain so even after fungus is killed.	**Nontoxic:** water wash, antitranspirant spray **Contact:** folpet, fenarimol **Systemic:** benomyl, triadimefon, triforine
Rust	Small orange spots enlarge into thick, powdery masses of orange spores on leaf undersides; yellow blotches appear on leaf surfaces. Severe infection can defoliate a plant.	**Nontoxic:** none **Contact:** chlorothalonil **Systemic:** benomyl, oxycarboxin, triadimefon, triforine

Pruning—Theory & Practice

The objectives of pruning are simple: to promote a symmetrical bush, to encourage new growth, and to remove any diseased, damaged, or dead wood. Yet over the years, no other aspect of rose culture has aroused so much controversy. For more than half a century, battle lines were drawn between the advocates of light pruning and those who championed hard cutting back. Today, a better understanding of plant physiology and rose ancestries, coupled with extensive trial-and-error data, has revealed that light-to-moderate pruning produces the best possible garden plants and plenty of good flowers.

How a plant grows

The roots, stems, and leaves of a rose all work together for the plant's continued growth and productivity. Roots, of course, not only anchor the plant in the soil, but also absorb nutrients which are carried upward and throughout the stems in specialized cells. At the same time, leaves take in carbon dioxide from the atmosphere, converting it into sugars and other "foods" which are transported throughout the plant in another type of specialized cell.

Not all absorbed nutrients and synthesized substances (such as sugars and proteins) are used immediately; some are stored for later use in the tissues of roots and stems. For example, proteins are stockpiled in the wood and bark cells during the end of the growing season, then used by the plant early in spring, before leaves are present to manufacture the compounds needed for renewed growth.

Because roses store so much energy in their canes, heavy pruning imposes several hardships. In throwing away stems, you throw away many of the resources reserved for spring growth—and that forces the plant to rely upon reserves in the roots for the initial growth push. And since the root system enlarges in proportion to the size of the plant, continual heavy pruning results in a small root system with correspondingly small amounts of stored nutrients. Finally, heavily pruned plants produce a more limited amount of growth at first flush than do lightly or moderately pruned bushes, and thus have fewer leaves available to synthesize nutrients for new growth.

Timing & tools

For most modern roses, the best time to prune is toward the end of the dormant season, when growth buds along the canes begin to swell. Where winter temperatures are mild, this can be as early as January, but in the "icebox" regions of the northeast, central, and mountain states, you won't think about it until late March or April. In general, you should prune in winter or early spring, but not so early that the new growth which follows will be caught by late frosts.

In areas where winter lingers and chilly days alternate with more springlike weather during the transitional months of March or April, gardeners often use two indicators to determine pruning time. Thirty days before the last expected killing frost is generally a safe time (your County Cooperative Extension Advisor can give you an average date). You can also assume the time is ripe when forsythia comes into bloom.

To prune your roses well, you need two tools: sharp pruning shears and a pruning saw. The shears will take care of most of the work, but a small keyhole or coping saw is required for removing larger canes and those in areas that are awkward for shears.

How to prune hybrid teas, grandifloras & floribundas

Regardless of where you live, the following guidelines should help you prune any of the popular modern bush roses: hybrid teas, grandifloras, and floribundas. (Additional tips for miniatures, climbers, and shrub and old garden roses are on page 88 to 89.)

■ Remove all dead wood and all weak, twiggy branches. If an older cane produced nothing but weak growth, remove it at the bud union.

■ Open up the bush by removing all branches that cross through the center. This gives you a "vase-shaped" plant (a slender or fat vase, depending on how upright or spreading the variety grows) without a central profusion of twigs and leaves where insects and diseases could hide out and flourish. *Note:* Rosarians in very hot climates often just shorten branches crossing through the center. These will produce enough leaves to shield canes thoroughly from the scorching sun.

■ Remove up to one-third the length of all new growth for the past year. (However, to develop really large specimen shrubs in the mild-winter areas of the South and West, don't cut into live new growth of the past season that is much thicker than a pencil.)

If you use a winter protection method that requires reducing the bush size to fit the protector, you will almost surely remove more than one-third of the past year's growth. In this case, try not to reduce the height any further in spring. You will, however, need to cut out *all* damaged and winter-killed wood, regardless of how low this leaves your bushes.

■ Make all cuts above a leaf bud that points toward the outside of the plant.

■ Paint all cuts made through canes thicker than lead-pencil size (and particularly all cuts to the bud union) with a sealing compound. The white glue that comes in small plastic bottles with dispenser tops is easy to use and entirely satisfactory for this purpose: just squeeze one to several drops of glue onto the cut surface and spread it out to cover

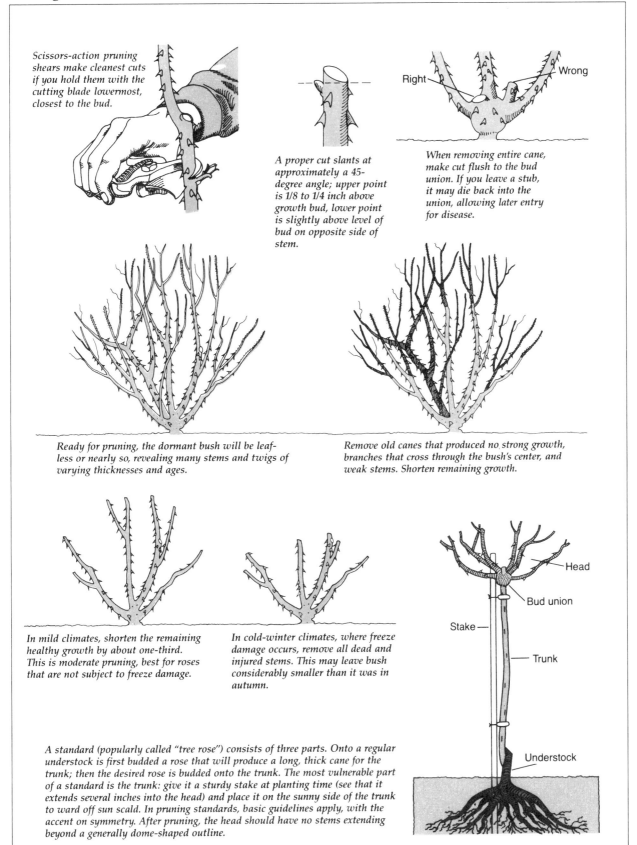

Scissors-action pruning shears make cleanest cuts if you hold them with the cutting blade lowermost, closest to the bud.

A proper cut slants at approximately a 45-degree angle; upper point is 1/8 to 1/4 inch above growth bud, lower point is slightly above level of bud on opposite side of stem.

Right

Wrong

When removing entire cane, make cut flush to the bud union. If you leave a stub, it may die back into the union, allowing later entry for disease.

Ready for pruning, the dormant bush will be leafless or nearly so, revealing many stems and twigs of varying thicknesses and ages.

Remove old canes that produced no strong growth, branches that cross through the bush's center, and weak stems. Shorten remaining growth.

In mild climates, shorten the remaining healthy growth by about one-third. This is moderate pruning, best for roses that are not subject to freeze damage.

In cold-winter climates, where freeze damage occurs, remove all dead and injured stems. This may leave bush considerably smaller than it was in autumn.

Head

Bud union

Stake

Trunk

Understock

A standard (popularly called "tree rose") consists of three parts. Onto a regular understock is first budded a rose that will produce a long, thick cane for the trunk; then the desired rose is budded onto the trunk. The most vulnerable part of a standard is the trunk: give it a sturdy stake at planting time (see that it extends several inches into the head) and place it on the sunny side of the trunk to ward off sun scald. In pruning standards, basic guidelines apply, with the accent on symmetry. After pruning, the head should have no stems extending beyond a generally dome-shaped outline.

◆ *Pruning*

the cut. Where rose cane borer is a problem, many rosarians cover all pruning wounds to prevent entry of borers.

■ Be on the lookout for suckers, often appearing as long, slender, flexible canes from below the bud union. If you find a sucker, *pull* it down and off the plant. Merely cutting it off will leave undeveloped growth eyes at the sucker's base that will produce more suckers in the future.

How to prune miniature roses

At the end of the dormant season, cut back miniature plants to the lowest outward-facing growth eyes on the previous season's stems; this leaves you with a severely pruned plant that will produce the strongest new growth for flower production. If you hesitate to prune so heavily, be sure to cut plants back by at least half, removing all weak and twiggy growth. During the growth season, remove faded blooms, cutting the stems back by about half. If any long, rank growth occurs, pinch or cut it back to promote branching.

How to prune climbing roses

Several distinct growth and flowering habits fall under the category of "climbing rose." What they all have in common is long, flexible canes that produce flowers from eyes along their length.

Climbing hybrid teas & large-flowered climbers.
After you plant one of these climbers, leave it unpruned for the next 2 or 3 years: it takes a while for plants to become established. During this period, just remove all dead canes and branches, weak growth, and spent flowers; tie new canes into position as they mature (see facing page).

In several years, the plant will consist solely of long canes produced after you planted it in your garden—and from these canes will come the side branches (laterals) that bear flowers. Varieties differ in how they produce the canes; some types throw out new canes from the base each year, while others build up a more woody structure and produce most long new canes from higher on the plant.

In pruning climbers, your objectives are twofold: to encourage growth of more flowering laterals and to stimulate production of new canes that will gradually replace the older, less productive ones. Don't cut back the long canes at all unless any of them grows too long for the allotted space. And whenever long canes or branches grow in the wrong direction, first try to train them into place; only if this doesn't work should you remove them entirely.

For annual pruning, remove only the old and obviously unproductive wood. Then cut back to two or three eyes all of the laterals that bore flowers during the last year. The best blooms are produced on laterals growing from 2- or 3-year-old wood.

Large-flowered climbers that bloom only in spring should be pruned after flowering ends. At that time, cut out the least productive old canes and any weak, old, or tangled branches. New canes will grow from the base and low down on the remaining canes, and strong new laterals will grow from farther out on the older canes that you leave. From this new growth come most of the branches that will carry next year's flowers. Little good is done by removing spent flower clusters—some varieties may produce secondary blooms from the midst of old flower clusters or just below them, and many go on to develop colorful hips.

Pillar roses. Two sorts of climbing roses are grown as flowering pillars up to about 10 feet tall. One is the hybrid tea or floribunda climber which grows short (8- to 10-foot) climbing canes. The other is a natural pillar type which grows upright, 6- to 10-foot canes that will flower along their length. Pruning objectives and methods are the same as for climbing hybrid teas; the principal difference is that you will train long new growth upright.

Rambler roses. These climbers cover themselves with clusters of small to medium-size flowers in late spring, then produce many long, limber canes from ground level and a lesser number of long laterals from growth that has flowered. The next year's blooms come from this new growth.

Wait to prune ramblers until flowering has ended and new growth has begun. Cut out canes that have just flowered and show no sign of producing any long, vigorous new shoots. As the new canes lengthen and mature, train them into position.

Pruning shrub & old garden roses

The durable and venerable rose species and old varieties represent such a diversity of types and growth habits that it is difficult to generalize about them. Most, however, are vigorous growers that may need some thinning and shaping each year but little actual cutting back. Since most of these roses are used as specimen shrubs or hedges, the primary pruning should be directed toward trimming and shaping them to fit into the landscape picture. Cut back any shoots that depart unattractively from the general pattern of the plant; remove any weak wood and any old canes that produced little new growth or flowers.

You can prune the repeat-flowering individuals at the same time you would hybrid teas. However, when pruning once-blooming shrub and old garden roses, wait until they finish flowering, then cut out the least productive old wood. You may also shorten any especially long new canes; this will encourage them to put forth a greater number of flowering laterals.

Some old roses—especially many hybrid perpetuals—produce fairly long, arching canes in the manner of climbing roses. And like climbers, they bloom more heavily if the canes are trained horizontally or arched over and the tips "pegged" to the ground.

Left to its own devices, a long climbing cane will continue to build new tissues to increase only its steady upward growth. This is an example of *apical dominance:* the topmost growth continues at the expense of any lateral growth. When a long, upright cane is arched over or bent down to a horizontal position, however, the apex of growth is thwarted—and many eyes along the cane will begin to grow, each one heading upward. These laterals are the growth that gives you flowers.

If you have a high fence, wall, or house side to cover, let the vertical canes grow to about 10 feet long. Then lean them out at an angle from the plant's base on both sides of the plant. Tie canes horizontally and space them 1½ to 2 feet apart, paralleling one above the other. Arch the end of each cane downward and tie it in place.

Climbers trained horizontally along a low fence or wall will tend to produce flowering shoots from most eyes in the horizontal portions of the canes.

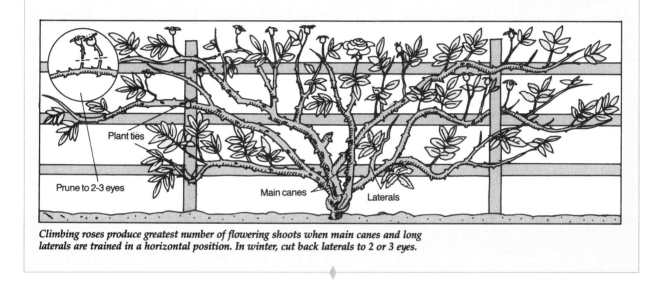

Climbing roses produce greatest number of flowering shoots when main canes and long laterals are trained in a horizontal position. In winter, cut back laterals to 2 or 3 eyes.

Pruning aftercare

A thorough rose garden clean-up should be a basic part of your annual routine, and the easiest time to do the job is immediately after pruning. First, remove any leaves that remain on your rose plants. Next, rake up and discard all old leaves, prunings, and any other debris on the ground or around the bases of the bushes; insect eggs and some disease spores may be carried from one year to the next on old or dead foliage.

Right after cleaning the rose beds, spray the pruned bushes and the ground around them as a final hedge against insect eggs and disease spores that may have remained on the plants or the soil's surface. Lime-sulfur (calcium polysulfide) or a lime-sulfur and oil combination are the traditional dormant clean-up sprays and must be used while roses are completely dormant. Simpler to apply (and every bit as effective) during the cold of late winter or early spring is a combination insecticide-fungicide made up of sprays normally used during the growing season. Such a dormant spray can be applied safely even after new growth has begun to emerge.

Other ways to regulate growth

After new growth is underway in early spring, check over the emerging new shoots to see what directions they're taking; then break or rub out any that are poorly located or unnecessary (crossing through the center of the bush, for example). Sometimes two or three new shoots will grow from one leaf axil. When you notice this, carefully rub out all but the strongest one.

During the flowering season, you will be removing flowers from your bushes—some for decoration in the house, the rest just to tidy up the plants. When you want a few long-stemmed beauties for inside, cut each stem so that you leave *at least* two sets of leaves on the branch from which you cut the flower. When you remove faded blooms from the bushes, cut down only as far as necessary to keep the bush well shaped—usually to the first five-leaflet leaf that points away from the bush's center.

New rose bushes and weak or small plants that you're trying to build up need all possible leaves to manufacture nutrients. Just snap the faded flowers from these plants— don't cut blossoms with stems for the house.

Winter Protection

Generally speaking, modern bush and climbing roses will withstand temperatures down to 10°F/–12°C unprotected. Even among modern roses, though, there's considerable variation in hardiness; for example, many yellow, orange, and bronze-toned types are more tender than the average. Floribundas and hybrid perpetuals are usually more cold tolerant than the hybrid teas. Most shrub and old garden roses can make it on their own until the temperature drops to –10°F/–23°C; many species, species hybrids, and certain shrub roses can take much lower readings.

Tips for winter survival

Contrary to what you might expect, one purpose of winter protection is to keep roses constantly *cold*, not warm.

In itself, low temperature is far less harmful to roses than are sudden, rapid, or frequent *changes* in temperature. Because moisture in the canes expands when it freezes, quick freezes break cell walls inside canes and destroy vital plant tissue. Repeated bouts of freezing, thawing, and refreezing can ruin exposed canes. What you want are thoroughly dormant canes at a fairly constant temperature—ideally in the 15° to 25°F/–9° to –4°C range.

Another winter stress to guard against is desiccation. Cold winds dry out exposed canes, and if the soil is frozen, roots cannot take up water to replace the lost moisture. Moreover, if the canes have suffered any cold damage, the injured cells can't resist water loss. In spring, you'll find shriveled, blackened canes instead of plump, green wood.

Winter protection begins at planting time, since location and exposure influence the intensity of cold and amount of temperature fluctuation. Cold air seeks the lowest level, so valley gardens will be colder than those on surrounding hillsides. Similarly, low pockets in your garden will be consistently chillier than elevated or sloping areas. Roses planted in such low spots are in greater danger of freezing at the bud union unless well insulated; they're also more vulnerable to any late freezes.

Winter winds are often distinctly colder than still air—the "wind chill factor" mentioned by meteorologists. Thus, plantings sheltered from wind—whether by walls, other shrubbery and trees, or your house—are likely to be warmer than exposed plantings and will suffer less from desiccation. Climbing roses may survive in regions normally beyond their range if planted against a house or garage wall that provides wind protection and raises (by means of reflected heat) the overall low temperature.

Care during the growing season also has a great influence on potential cold tolerance. Plants maintained in vigorous good health throughout the past year and not defoliated by disease or insects stand a much better chance than weaklings that have just managed to scrape by.

It's also important to adjust your care so that plants will be "mature"—not still actively growing and blooming—when the first frosts occur. Cells in growing stems and canes have high moisture and low starch contents; this makes them more susceptible to freezing and cell damage. In contrast, mature growth has a much higher percentage of solids to moisture. By withholding nitrogen fertilizers about 6 weeks before expected frosts (see "When to stop," page 81) and allowing September blooms to stay on the plants and form hips, you'll help bring your roses to a well-ripened state—ready to face several months of cold.

Preparation & protection

No matter what form of winter protection you decide to use, there are some basic guidelines to follow. First, clear all old leaves and spent flowers from the rose bed and remove all debris and mulch from around the base of each plant. Next, strip away any foliage remaining on the canes. Leaves left on the plant will continue to lose moisture and may harbor disease organisms over the winter; and if the plants are kept under protective cones (see facing page), the leaves may decay and spread disease to the canes. As a final step—right before you expect the ground to freeze—give your bushes one last deep soaking (you can do this after mounding soil around the bases).

Though winter protection can make the difference between survival and death, you shouldn't put it in place too soon. Mound soil over plant bases in early autumn, but wait until the soil freezes to apply mulch over the mounds. If you use cold frames, mound the bushes in early autumn and put the frame sides in place at your convenience, but wait until you expect a temperature of 15° to 25°F/–9° to –4°C before putting on the roof. During warm spells in winter, raise the lid for ventilation. Styrofoam cones should go in place after the first freeze (plants having been mounded earlier) but while you still can dig the soil to cover the cone bases. For better health of the rose inside, cut a 1-inch diameter ventilation hole at the top of each of a cone's four sides. And if the cone has a solid top, cut it off (or out) to make a lid for ventilating during warm spells.

For roses protected by soil mounds or open-topped cylinders alone, cut canes back to about 3 feet high and tie them together to keep them from whipping about in winter winds.

Uncovering in spring

Early springtime weather is often unpredictable: any number of times before spring arrives for good, warm weather suddenly turns freezing, then warms up again. Don't be tempted by the first breath of spring to remove cold frames and rose cones; just open the roof or top on warm, sunny days, but close it if freezes are predicted. If you protect only with soil mounds, gradually begin to remove soil when it thaws. Do this carefully to avoid breaking any growth that may have begun under the mound.

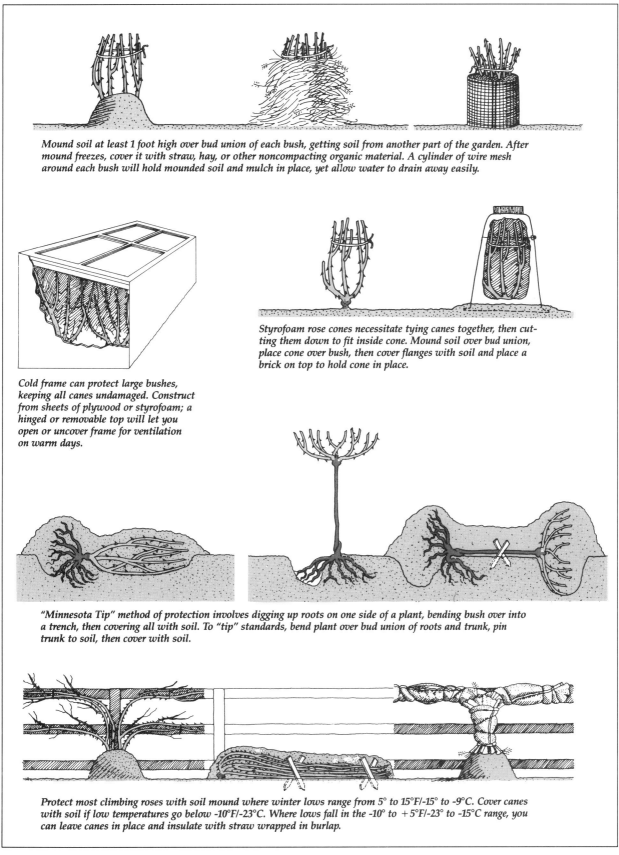

Mound soil at least 1 foot high over bud union of each bush, getting soil from another part of the garden. After mound freezes, cover it with straw, hay, or other noncompacting organic material. A cylinder of wire mesh around each bush will hold mounded soil and mulch in place, yet allow water to drain away easily.

Cold frame can protect large bushes, keeping all canes undamaged. Construct from sheets of plywood or styrofoam; a hinged or removable top will let you open or uncover frame for ventilation on warm days.

Styrofoam rose cones necessitate tying canes together, then cutting them down to fit inside cone. Mound soil over bud union, place cone over bush, then cover flanges with soil and place a brick on top to hold cone in place.

"Minnesota Tip" method of protection involves digging up roots on one side of a plant, bending bush over into a trench, then covering all with soil. To "tip" standards, bend plant over bud union of roots and trunk, pin trunk to soil, then cover with soil.

Protect most climbing roses with soil mound where winter lows range from 5° to 15°F/-15° to -9°C. Cover canes with soil if low temperatures go below -10°F/-23°C. Where lows fall in the -10° to +5°F/-23° to -15°C range, you can leave canes in place and insulate with straw wrapped in burlap.

Propagation

The chief reason for propagating your own roses is simply the pleasure of it. Words can't describe the satisfaction provided by beautiful blooms on a rose plant that *you* nurtured from a scrap of wood. Of course, if you want more plants of a rose that's no longer sold, or of one you can't identify, then you'll have to grow your own from cuttings or by budding. If you have the creative urge (and a bit of the gambler's spirit), you can also try raising new roses from seed.

New plants from cuttings

You can start cuttings from softwood during the blooming season or from dormant wood (hardwood) at pruning time.

For softwood cuttings, follow the steps illustrated, starting with stems that have just flowered. To keep the leaves from wilting, enclose the entire pot in a plastic bag or invert a glass jar over it. Bag-covered cuttings shouldn't need any additional water during the rooting period, but if you use a jar, check often to make sure the rooting medium doesn't dry out. In a month or two, when new growth shows that the cutting has rooted, you can remove the bag or jar.

For hardwood cuttings, make pencil-thick cuttings of dormant wood about 8 inches long. Remove the two lowest eyes, dip the end to be rooted in a rooting hormone powder, and insert it 3 to 4 inches deep in a pot or the ground. To plant it in the ground, dig a trench, place ½ to 1 inch of coarse sand in the bottom, and fill in around the cuttings with a half-and-half blend of sand and soil. To start cuttings in pots, use a light, sandy potting soil.

Cuttings from New Growth

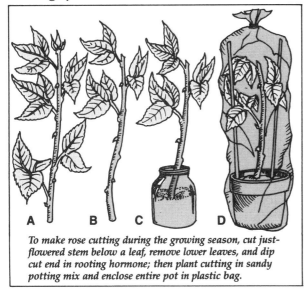

To make rose cutting during the growing season, cut just-flowered stem below a leaf, remove lower leaves, and dip cut end in rooting hormone; then plant cutting in sandy potting mix and enclose entire pot in plastic bag.

New plants by budding

Most bare-root rose bushes are budded plants propagated by the method shown on the facing page. Commercial understocks are selected for good root systems that are easy to dig and ship: two of the most widely used types are *Rosa multiflora*, a species from Japan, and the semi-double, maroon-red climber 'Dr. Huey'. Multiflora is preferred for colder climates; 'Dr. Huey' is better for mild-winter regions.

For at-home budding, your understock need only root easily and accept the majority of the buds you put on it. One ready source of understocks is sucker growth from budded plants. In addition, old rambler types 'American Pillar', 'Crimson Rambler', 'Dorothy Perkins', and 'Veilchenblau' have been successful. If you live in a mild-winter area, you might also try *Rosa banksiae* and 'Climbing Cecile Brunner'.

Prepare and root the cuttings as described for hardwood cuttings (at left)—but gouge out all but the top two growth eyes to discourage possible sucker growth below the bud. The budding operation will be simpler if you root the understock cuttings in containers, since you can then bud at table height rather than ground level.

Spring and summer are the seasons for budding, since the understock must be succulent enough that its bark peels back easily from the stem. You can buy special budding knives with the very sharp, clean-cutting edge you need; some come with flattened handles that are designed to lift the bark flaps formed by the T cut.

To tie the bud in place, you can use a variety of items, all sold at horticultural supply houses: plastic tape, budding rubber (5- to 8-inch strips like wide rubber bands), or, simplest of all, plastic bud coverings—patches that completely cover a bud and clip together on the opposite side of the stem.

About 3 to 4 weeks after budding, you should see evidence of success or failure. If the bud is plump and green, you have the start of a new rose bush. If it's black and shriveled, try another bud a bit lower on the opposite side of the same understock.

New plants from seeds

Rose breeders wanting to produce totally new rose varieties pollinate one rose variety from another and grow hybrid plants from the resulting seeds. The activity is known as hybridizing and can be an engaging pastime for the home rose grower as well.

At first you may want to plant seeds from hips that form naturally. Until the mid-19th century most new roses came from such unplanned crosses. Doing this will give you the experience of harvesting, planting, and raising new plants with the minimum of disappointment should any fatalities occur. The blooms on these seedlings are likely to spur you on to planning and making definite crosses—either because they are so fascinating or because they are so nondescript that you feel a little guidance is needed!

Budding, Step by Step

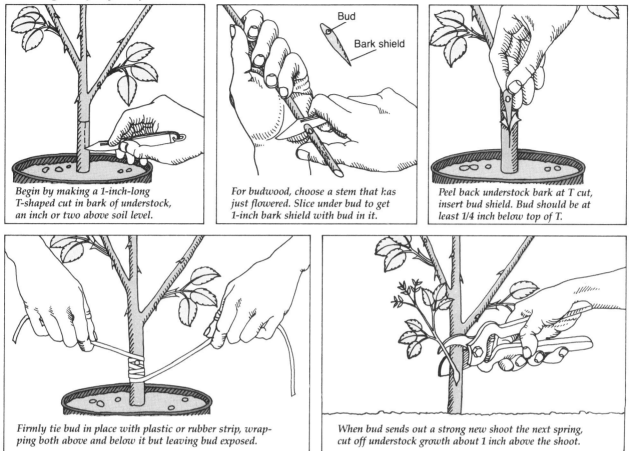

Begin by making a 1-inch-long T-shaped cut in bark of understock, an inch or two above soil level.

Bud
Bark shield

For budwood, choose a stem that has just flowered. Slice under bud to get 1-inch bark shield with bud in it.

Peel back understock bark at T cut, insert bud shield. Bud should be at least 1/4 inch below top of T.

Firmly tie bud in place with plastic or rubber strip, wrapping both above and below it but leaving bud exposed.

When bud sends out a strong new shoot the next spring, cut off understock growth about 1 inch above the shoot.

How to Hybridize a Rose

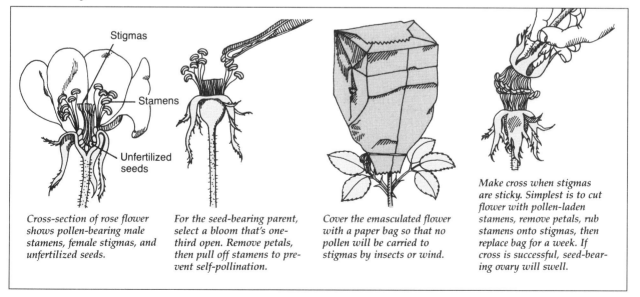

Stigmas

Stamens

Unfertilized seeds

Cross-section of rose flower shows pollen-bearing male stamens, female stigmas, and unfertilized seeds.

For the seed-bearing parent, select a bloom that's one-third open. Remove petals, then pull off stamens to prevent self-pollination.

Cover the emasculated flower with a paper bag so that no pollen will be carried to stigmas by insects or wind.

Make cross when stigmas are sticky. Simplest is to cut flower with pollen-laden stamens, remove petals, rub stamens onto stigmas, then replace bag for a week. If cross is successful, seed-bearing ovary will swell.

◆ Propagation

Where frosts come in October, do all hybridizing with the first crop of bloom in spring. Hips need about 4 months to form, mature, and ripen; they're ready for picking when they turn orange, yellow, or brown.

Germination is generally more successful if you give the hips an after-ripening period of low (but not freezing) temperatures in a moist atmosphere. To accomplish this, just place ripe hips in boxes or plastic bags, cover them with damp peat moss, vermiculite, or sand, and place them in the crisper bin of your refrigerator. By December or January, the hips will be black and partially decomposed; remove them from the refrigerator at that time and shell out the seeds. These will be of odd sizes and shapes, but a convenient indicator of which are good and which aren't is the water test: plant those that sink in water, discard those that float.

Planting the seeds. In a lightweight, sterile potting soil, plant seeds ⅜ to ½ inch deep. You can plant closely in shallow containers, then transplant seedlings to larger containers (or small individual pots) when they have their first set of true leaves; or you can plant seeds about 2 inches apart in deeper (at least 3-inch deep) pots and let them flower without transplanting. Germination may begin within 6 weeks of planting and continue for about 2 months; some seeds that fail to germinate during this period may grow the next year.

Growing the seedlings. In mild-winter regions, you can plant seeds and raise seedlings outdoors. But in colder areas, an indoor start—in a greenhouse, on a sunny window sill, or under artificial light—will let seedlings come into bloom early, then give them the full growing season to develop. A bush hybrid tea seedling may bloom as early as six weeks from germination (climbers and old rose seedlings may take 2-3 years), so cold-climate gardeners can flower rose seedlings during winter and early spring before roses outside even have new growth. As soon as spring frost danger is past, you can move your seedlings outside. Protect them from wind and direct sunlight for about a week, until they adjust to the outdoor atmosphere.

If you wish to try artificial lights, use the 40-watt fluorescent tubes made especially for growing indoor plants. A two-tube fixture is satisfactory, but a four-tube set-up is preferable because of its better light distribution. Position the lights about 6 inches above the containers, and leave them on for 16 hours each day.

Damping-off fungus can rot young seedlings at soil level or even before they emerge. Planting in sterile potting mix will help you avoid this problem, and as further precaution, you can dust seeds with the fungicide captan before planting. Should damping-off develop, water the seedlings with a fungicide solution containing captan, thiram, or zineb. Watch young seedlings closely for mildew and control it as needed.

Roses Go Public

Given the rose's tremendous popularity, it's hardly a surprise that so many public gardens across the United States feature roses prominently—or even exclusively. Such gardens take you a step beyond photographs and written descriptions, showing you what a given rose *really* looks like and letting you rate its performance under local conditions and in comparison to others of its kind. Many public gardens make a concerted effort to add new varieties each year; those that are official AARS test gardens (page 62) are certain to be furnished with up-to-the-minute introductions.

The listings here constitute a representative sampling of fine public rose gardens, sure to inspire and inform the novice rosarian.

ALABAMA
Mobile
Battleship Memorial Park
Springdale Plaza Park

Theodore
Bellingrath Gardens

ARIZONA
Phoenix
Valley Garden Center Rose Garden

Tucson
Gene C. Reid Park

ARKANSAS
Little Rock
Arkansas State Capitol Garden

CALIFORNIA
Berkeley
Berkeley Municipal Rose Garden

Citrus Heights
Fountain Square Garden

La Cañada
Descanso Gardens

Los Angeles
Exposition Park

Oakland
Morcum Amphitheater of Roses

Pasadena
Wrigley Gardens

Sacramento
Capitol Park

San Diego
Parker Garden at Balboa Park

San Francisco
Golden Gate Park Rose Garden

San Jose
San Jose Municipal Garden

San Marino
Huntington Botanical Gardens

Santa Barbara
City Rose Garden

Whittier
Rose Hills Memorial Park

COLORADO
Littleton
War Memorial Garden

Longmont
Lions Club Memorial Garden

CONNECTICUT
Norwich
Norwich Memorial Garden

West Hartford
Elizabeth Park Rose Garden

FLORIDA
Cypress Gardens
Florida Cypress Gardens

Lake Buena Vista
Walt Disney World

GEORGIA
Athens
Elizabeth Turner Rose Garden,
  University of Georgia

Atlanta
Greater Atlanta Rose Garden,
  Piedmont Park

Thomasville
Thomasville Rose Test Garden

HAWAII
Kula, Maui
University of Hawaii, Maui
  Agricultural Research Center

Honolulu, Oahu
Queen Kapiolani Park

ILLINOIS
Alton
Nan Elliott Memorial Garden,
  Moore Community Park

Evanston
Merrick Park Rose Garden

Libertyville
Cook Memorial Park

Peoria
Glen Oak Botanical Garden

Rockford
Sinnissippi Garden

Springfield
Washington Park Rose Garden

Wheaton
Cantigny

INDIANA

Fort Wayne
Lakeside Garden

Richmond
E.G. Hill Memorial Rose Garden

IOWA

Ames
Iowa State University,
  Horticultural Gardens

Bettendorf
Bettendorf Park Rose Garden

Cedar Rapids
Noelridge Park Rose Garden

Davenport
Vander Veer Park Rose Garden

Des Moines
Greenwood Park Rose Garden

Muscatine
Weed Park Memorial Rose Garden

State Center
State Center Rose Garden

KANSAS

Topeka
E.F.A. Reinisch Rose Garden

KENTUCKY

Louisville
Kentucky Memorial Rose Garden,
  Kentucky Exposition Center

LOUISIANA

Baton Rouge
Louisiana State University,
  Rose Test Garden

Many
Hodges Gardens

Shreveport
The American Rose Center

MAINE

Portland
Deering Oaks Park Rose Circle

MARYLAND

Wheaton
Brookside Gardens

MASSACHUSETTS

Boston
James P. Kelleher Rose Garden

Westfield
Stanley Park of Westfield

MICHIGAN

East Lansing
Michigan State University,
  Horticulture Gardens

Lansing
Frances Park Memorial Garden

Wayne
Wayne County Cooperative
  Extension Garden

MINNESOTA

Minneapolis
Lake Harriet Rose Garden

MISSISSIPPI

Hattiesburg
Hattiesburg Area Rose Garden,
  University of Southern
  Mississippi

MISSOURI

Cape Girardeau
Capaha Park Rose Display Garden

Kansas City
Laura Conyers Smith Rose Garden

St. Louis
Missouri Botanical Gardens

MONTANA

Missoula
Missoula Memorial Rose Garden

NEBRASKA

Lincoln
Lincoln Municipal Rose Garden,
  Antelope Park

Omaha
Memorial Park Rose Garden

West Omaha
Boys Town Rose Garden

NEVADA

Reno
Reno Municipal Rose Garden

NEW JERSEY

Bloomfield
Brookdale Park Rose Garden

East Millstone
Rudolf W. van der Goot Rose
  Garden

Lincroft
Lambertus C. Bobbink Memorial
  Garden

Tenafly
Jack D. Lissemore Rose Garden,
  Davis Johnson Park

NEW MEXICO

Albuquerque
Prospect Park Rose Garden

NEW YORK

Bronx
Edwin De T. Bechtel Memorial Rose
  Garden, New York Botanical
  Garden

Brooklyn
Cranford Memorial Rose Garden,
  Brooklyn Botanic Gardens

Canandaigua
Sonnenberg Gardens

Flushing
Queens Botanical Garden

New York
United Nations Rose Garden

Old Westbury
Old Westbury Gardens

Rochester
Maplewood Park Garden

Schenectady
Central Park Rose Garden

Syracuse
Dr. Edmund B. Mills Rose Garden,
  Thorndon Park

NORTH CAROLINA

Asheville
Biltmore House and Gardens

Clemmons
Tanglewood Park Rose Garden

Fayetteville
Fayetteville Rose Garden,
  Fayetteville Technical Institute

Raleigh
Raleigh Municipal Rose Garden

Winston-Salem
Reynolda Rose Gardens of Wake
  Forest University

OHIO

Akron
Stan Hywett Hall and Gardens

Columbus
Columbus Park of Roses

Mansfield
Kingwood Center, Charles Edwin
  Nall Memorial Garden

OKLAHOMA

Muskogee
J.E. Conard Municipal Garden,
  Honor Heights Park

Oklahoma City
Municipal Rose Garden,
  Will Rogers Park

Tulsa
Tulsa Municipal Rose Garden,
  Woodward Park

OREGON

Coos Bay
Shore Acres State Park

Corvallis
Corvallis Rose Garden

Eugene
George E. Owen Municipal Garden

Portland
International Rose Test Garden

PENNSYLVANIA

Allentown
Malcolm W. Gross Memorial Rose
  Garden

Hershey
Hershey Rose Gardens

Kennett Square
Longwood Gardens

Philadelphia
Merion W. Rivinus Rose Garden

West Grove
Robert Pyle Memorial Rose Garden

SOUTH CAROLINA

Orangeburg
Edisto Memorial Gardens

TENNESSEE

Chattanooga
Warner Park Rose Garden

Memphis
Memphis Municipal Rose Garden,
  Audubon Park

TEXAS

Dallas
Samuell-Grand Rose Garden

El Paso
El Paso Municipal Rose Garden

Fort Worth
Fort Worth Botanic Garden

Houston
Houston Municipal Rose Garden

Orange
Brown Center Rose Garden,
  Lamar University

Tyler
Tyler Municipal Rose Garden

UTAH

Fillmore
Territorial Statehouse Rose Garden

Nephi
Nephi Memorial Rose Garden

Salt Lake City
Salt Lake City Municipal Rose
  Garden, Sugar House Park

VIRGINIA

Arlington
Arlington Memorial Rose Garden,
  Bon Air Park

Alexandria
American Horticultural Society,
  River Farm Garden

Norfolk
Bicentennial Rose Garden, Norfolk
  Botanical Gardens

WASHINGTON

Bellingham
Fairhaven Park Rose Garden

Chehalis
Chehalis Municipal Rose Garden

Seattle
Woodland Park Rose Garden

Spokane
Manito Park, Rosehill

Tacoma
Point Defiance Park Rose Garden

WEST VIRGINIA

Huntington
Ritter Park Garden

WISCONSIN

Hales Corners
Boerner Botanical Gardens,
  Whitnall Park

Index—General Subject Matter

Index—Rose Varieties